Nature's God

By Steve Wunsch

Table of Contents

1. The Laws of Nature and of Nature's God

This is a call to network scientists for help. The United States and other Western democracies have lost their attachment to property as the guiding principle of society. These governments have become primarily vehicles for redistributing property from one group to another and, as a consequence, their societies are disintegrating as groups contending for the property distributions wage intellectual and moral war against one another.

Network science can help. With economic collapse a daily threat, the remedies orchestrated by government have led only to a parade of failures. The common thread in these failures is redistribution. It is both the cause of and the supposed remedy for every problem. It is the subtext of every position, every proposal, every negotiation, every vote, and every election. Redistribution is deemed to be the one essential role of modern governments, although it has never resulted in anything but social conflict and economic failure. Network science can cut this Gordian knot by demonstrating that redistribution is never wise, and might not even be feasible in practice.

First, as network scientists know, the concept they call *rich get richer* or *preferential attachment* drives network formation throughout the universe. Simply describing this natural force more fully may help us rethink the premises that are causing so much conflict. Seeing that nodes in a network discriminate in their attachments between rich and poor – between those with many links to others and those with few links to others – may lead to an understanding that neither discrimination nor inequality is an appropriate concern of government.

Second, an articulation of how network formation underlies industrial organization may cause a reexamination of the wisdom of antitrust. The assumption that governments can manage industries better than the private parties who built them will be easier to challenge if the industries are dissected from a network perspective both before and after the onset of regulation.

An examination of stock exchanges will be particularly fruitful in this regard. We are entering a period of rapidly escalating dysfunction in this field that is specifically identifiable as network related and clearly caused by antitrust. Since reforms were draconian in their network transformation consequences, it may be an opportune moment to explain the difference between *aristocratic* networks on the one hand, and *egalitarian* or *random* networks on the other, and why the former are associated with efficient organization and the latter with disruption and disintegration.

The truth is that antitrust just drags an economy down without doing any good whatsoever, killing jobs, growth, and hope for a better future for millions of people. And the pursuit of the antitrust chimera creates a perpetually expanding elite of lawyers, bureaucrats and politicians that prey on the people, aggrandizing their own wealth and power while producing nothing of value in return.

Inequality is a natural consequence of network formation in the ordinary course of social and commercial progress. It develops according to nothing more nefarious or illegitimate than the universal laws being discovered in this relatively new science of networks. Being offended by inequality is like being offended by gravity or the weather.

But whether the benefits are real or imagined, policies that even attempt to redistribute will always create conflict. Those whose wealth must be confiscated will say the amount is too large, no matter how small it is, while the recipients of the confiscated amount will say it is too small, no matter how large it is. No King Solomon, no president, no political party preaching balance or shared sacrifice can quell this conflict. There will always be rage and righteous indignation on all sides as long as redistribution is around.

Democracies that fail to respect or allow the continued development of an unalienable right to property risk disintegration under mob rule. Thomas Jefferson and the Framers of the American experiment in liberty understood such dangers well, and tried to head them off in their new nation's founding documents. Of all the principles enshrined in those documents, property was in practice the most important right under "the Laws of Nature and of Nature's God." [i] It is inconceivable that such language could be honestly interpreted to allow redistribution of property based on the shifting whims of 51% majorities, much less on the shifting whims of unelected bureaucrats.

Western nations are beginning to be torn apart as their governments allocate property to the noisiest mobs. So far this problem has been mitigated by the great wealth of these nations that benefited most from property rights. But with those rights undone now, and wealth rapidly draining away, it won't be long before the explosions and implosions begin. Network scientists may help us understand where we went wrong, hopefully before it is too late.

2. No Justice, No Peace!

It is a staple of Occupy Wall Street protesters that the high degree of wealth concentration in America today is illegitimate. That 40% of assets are controlled by the richest 1% is prima facie evidence in the protesters' view that inequality is an aberration caused by greed. Claiming to speak for the 99%, they want everyone to recognize a shared responsibility to counter rising inequality by, say, raising taxes on the rich.

Those who espouse such views often say we are all connected by only six degrees of separation, as if our small world implied a moral obligation to share the wealth, and not just as voluntary charity, but pursuant to government-mandated redistribution. Interestingly, the same network science behind the six-degrees surprise has something to say about economic inequality, too. And it is not that inequality is an aberration caused by greed.

Small worlds happen because some nodes in a network become super-connectors, hubs that are attached to far more nodes than the others. Why? Because nodes apparently prefer to attach to nodes with more connections, as opposed to nodes with fewer connections. Network scientists call it *preferential attachment* or, less formally, *rich get richer*, mostly in cases where the term is merely metaphorical because the cases have nothing to do with people or wealth. But even when it does refer to people and wealth, there may be nothing more sinister going on than when thousands of fireflies in the tropical rainforest of Papua, New Guinea flash on and off simultaneously at a rate of twice every three seconds. Such network formation phenomena, which are now being found in many large and small corners of the observable universe, only point toward "some general organizing tendency in nature." [ii]

The path to small-world science began when Vilfredo Pareto noted in 1906 that 80% of the land in Italy was owned by 20% of the people. He also saw that 80% of the peas in his garden were in 20% of the pods. Since then, the Pareto Principle, the 80-20 rule, has been confirmed many times in many places by many researchers. On the wealth inequality question, the results are in: it is everywhere. Every country in the world has inequality of wealth and income.

True, the United States may be the prime example of inequality today. [iii] But that is unquestionably a good thing for all Americans, including the 99%, because inequality and opportunity go hand in hand. Inequality has occurred primarily because the United States is more mature economically than other countries, and in particular because it has the largest stock market in the world, the very enterprise the Occupiers are upset about. Their ire aside, a stock market provides capital for jobs-creating companies, and is thus good for anyone wanting a job. But it also leads to widely diverging amounts of wealth, such as among company founders, average investors, and non-investors, assuring that wherever there is great wealth, there will be great inequality, too. This does not mean anything untoward created the great inequality in America. All it means is that the network formation process that leads to inequality has had more activity over which to work its small-world wonders in America than in other countries. It also means that achieving the

Occupiers' goal of less inequality would mean less wealth for everyone, and greater poverty for the poor.

When scientists observe what they suspect is a small-world network, they test their hypothesis by checking to see if it is governed by a *power law*. If it is, it will exhibit a regular relationship throughout the distribution between, for example, increases in wealth and decreases in the number of people with that level of wealth, a condition called *scale invariant* or *scale free*. Think of it as a ladder or one of the sides of a pyramid with steps. If it is straight, then it is as difficult to climb from the second step to the third step, as it is to climb from the tenth step to the eleventh step. If it meets this straightness test, then it is scale free and confirmed as having been generated by a power law. But the ladder or pyramid sides can be more or less steep, which could be thought of in the wealth context as the inequality gradient.

The power law generates distributions that don't look like the familiar bell curve, where most observations cluster around the average, and decreasing numbers of observations are spread out in the tails and eventually shrink to zero. Virtually everything people can see, touch and imagine, like height and weight, fits this bell curve pattern and is intuitively clear.

In contrast, scale-free networks are now being found to shape many aspects of our world in ways that are far different from the bell curve, and far from intuitively clear. To get a grip on the difference, consider what the distribution would look like if a power law drove the height of people. At the lower end, there could be billions of people less than three feet tall. Then there would be a regularly decreasing number of people at each taller level, until in the upper reaches of the distribution you might find a few giants that were hundreds of feet tall.

Human height, of course, is not driven by a power law. But wealth is. Graphing distributions of wealth always reveals scale free pyramids, for the whole world, and for every continent, region, country, state and city in the world. The primary reason the United States has such high and rising inequality is that the United States has been economically successful. But the pattern is common everywhere in the world, to one degree or another.

According to a 2011 Credit Suisse study, 38.5% of the world's wealth is controlled by 1% of the world's people. The inequality gradient steepened from the previous year as the top percent's share grew by 2.9% (from 35.6% to 38.5%). There are 2,700 people worth over $500 million; 29,000 people are worth $100 million to $500 million; 987,300 people are worth $10 million to $100 million; 1,959,600 people are worth $5 million to $10 million; and 26,724,200 people are worth $1 million to $5 million. [iv]

Perhaps the first surprise here is how many millionaires there are in the world, roughly 30 million of them (29,702,800, the sum of those worth over $1 million in the above groups), or about 0.42% of the 7 billion people in the world. The second surprise is how much inequality there is even amongst millionaires. 90% of all those worth at least $1 million are still relative paupers who haven't got $5 million to rub together (26,724,200/29,702,800=89.97%). So even at the top – and maybe especially at the top – there is plenty of motivation to improve one's condition through hard work and industry, as Adam Smith might say. Occupiers and the politicians who want to please them might object, saying fairness demands peeling off another few percent from those millionaires for redistribution purposes. After all, they have so much they wouldn't miss it anyway, right? But what if the incentives near the top are the most important of all, which, judging by their relative success so far, may well be the case? What if maintaining motivation among the successful is the key to sustaining innovation and growth in an economy?

In any case, this entire wealth-creating machine is in increasing danger from top to bottom, because it also provides plenty of motivation to attempt to subvert the natural structure by forcibly redistributing wealth downward. And there are plenty of politicians willing to play to this desire by appealing to the greater numbers of people at the lower income and wealth levels. Liberal Democrats, for example, often advocate spreading the wealth around and attempt to attract support by saying this is how democracy works. Think of them as members of the Blue Team.

With the Blue Team trying to redistribute wealth downward, the Red Team counters with its own arguments, creating loopholes, exemptions, favorable tax rates on capital gains, or dividends, or interest, or for politically favored investments – green jobs, ethanol, wind power, biotech, small businesses, municipal bonds, married families, children, first homes, second homes, etc. – often taking up the same causes the Blue Team champions, such as the middle class, to justify its positions. And the Red Team also likes to trot out the "that's how democracy works" line when political factions form over contentious issues. [v]

Both teams tout the notion that the fight to marshal a majority against the other team over redistribution is and should be the center of everyone's attention, never mind natural law or property rights. Both teams imply that mob rule is the essence of democracy, that moving property around based on whoever has the votes is what democracy is all about. It isn't just the Blue Team trying to hit the wealthy with higher taxes and the like, as is often the assumed case when the term "redistribution" is brought up in political debate. Such mentions are almost always in the context of a Red Team counter-redistribution argument, and it, too, is at heart a redistribution argument. In other words, class warfare goes both ways. It is not just the Blue Team that engages in it on behalf of the lower class. The Red Team is also fully engaged on behalf of the upper class. Class warfare is what all politicians do, and it is very nearly all they do.

Even so, a fundamental question must still be asked: Do attempts at redistribution actually work? Does all the fighting over votes and dividing things actually make a difference in wealth distribution? Surprisingly, the answer is less clear than the hullabaloo over redistribution politics would imply. Remember, the normal state of affairs is a really, really steep inequality gradient, which would translate to very, very unequal wealth. That being the case, it's just not all that easy to tell if the gradient added or dropped a "really," or inequality added or dropped a "very." In fact, it is in all likelihood impossible to say at any given point whether the Blue Team is winning or the Red Team is winning, whether the net effect of all the political maneuvering has resulted in an increase or a decrease in the normal wealth concentration proclivities of the power law.

Leading the troops in class warfare is good for political careers, which is why the politicians do it, of course. But there is little evidence that gains or losses on the redistribution battlefield really change things all that much. Inequality will tend to rise with economic success and fall with economic failure. It will contract in recessions and depressions – and especially during falling stock markets – and it will recover and expand with a rising economy and stock prices. But after all the progressive taxes on the one side and loopholes on the other, the rich will still be richer and fewer in number than the middle class or the poor. The distribution will still follow a scale invariant power law with a steep inequality gradient and "unfairness" everywhere you look.

This point is often lost as Blue Team analysts attribute inequality to the ebbs and flows of government actions rather than to economic fluctuations. The decline in inequality between the 1930s and the 1960s, for example, has been laid to the New Deal and progressive taxation, rather than to the Great Depression or its bear market companion. Similarly, increased inequality since then has been blamed on less progressivity or more loopholes or, more recently, bailouts, rather than on the massive growth of the last half-century. While government policies may have a transitory effect on equality, the studied avoidance of the obviously greater effects of economic growth or stock prices speaks to the primarily political purpose of such analyses. [vi]

The same point is also lost on the Red Team, which has its own rationales for redistribution. The Red Team supports small businesses ostensibly because in aggregate they hire a lot of people. But the truth is that the best thing about having lots of small businesses is that the chances are thereby increased that some of them will become big businesses. This is what really makes a dent in unemployment. But this fact is inconvenient for the Red Team, because advocating anything with the word "big" in it would be politically incorrect. So the Red Team happily confuses the issue with its small-business-is-beautiful-because-it-is-small message, thus chiming in with the Blue Team's anti-bigness message and sounding like just another believer in spreading the wealth around.

Both teams take these self-serving slants to imply they can reshape distribution outcomes. Both seek to maximize their perceived importance to changing the distribution picture so as to rally their own rabble. The Red Team's rabble knows that "small business" is code for low taxes on individuals and less progressivity. The Blue Team's rabble knows "balance" means higher taxes on the rich and more progressivity. But while both teams use a lot of code to imply where they stand, neither team is interested in the truth that distribution is pretty much unalterable by either of them.

The Office of Economic Cooperation and Development, a Paris-based global research organization funded by 34 member governments, [vii] is very anxious to prove that redistribution is good policy and is doable. But in spite of many attempts to prove these points to help the political class that funds the agency, it has never been able to prove either point. Although all governments have engaged in attempts at redistribution since 1980, according to OECD, inequality increased across the globe.

> In most countries the *extent* of redistribution has increased over the period as a whole. As a result, tax-benefit policies have offset some of the large

increases in market-income inequality but they appear to have become less effective at doing so over the past 10-15 years. Up until the mid-1990s, tax-benefit systems in many OECD countries offset more than half of the rise in market-income inequality. However, since then, while market-income inequality continued to rise, the stabilizing effect of taxes and benefits on household income inequality has mostly declined. In some countries, taxes and benefits became *less* redistributive during the last decade. [Emphasis in original.] [viii]

The implication for the Red and Blue teams is that, in the grand scheme, both are unimportant in terms of their main goal. So what do they do? Both take up confusion and disingenuous analysis as their underlying strategy. They gravitate toward whatever issues and presentations of them will generate the most heat and emotion in the class wars, regardless of objective truth or reality. To promote confusion, a favorite trick of both teams is the use of speeches or policies of the other team's ancestors, such as when the Red Team talks up the supply-side brilliance of the Kennedy tax cuts, or when the Blue Team praises Teddy Roosevelt for introducing big-business bashing, antitrust and progressivism to the modern American consciousness.

President Obama's State of the Union on January, 24, 2012 offered dozens of proposals in the interest of fairness and equality, from the Kennedyesque, "Ask yourselves what you can do to bring jobs back to your country, and your country will do everything we can to help you succeed," to egalitarian perennials, "Higher education can't be a luxury; it's an economic necessity that every American family should be able to afford," to "women should earn equal pay for equal work." Not to be outdone in his Republican response, Indiana governor Mitch Daniels offered a few programs of his own, focusing early and often for political correctness' sake on "equality," the "safety net" and popular entitlements Medicare and Social Security, and ceding the need for means testing "for the wealthiest among us" to receive benefits from such entitlements.

I harp on these charades to make the larger point that, without the potential to alter natural inequality, neither team would have anything to talk about. It is only because both teams fight over "change," which they both style as having plus or minus effects on their constituents' wealth, that they can recruit allies, money and political momentum to their redistributionist crusades. But there is no evidence that material changes in wealth distribution have been made through politics or have stuck for more than a fleeting moment. Even Communist countries have wealth pyramids and abundant inequality. [ix]

Unfortunately, our democracy today has adopted the mob rule version anyway. To make the difference clear, consider the following example. The Occupy Wall Street protesters took over a "private/public" square called Zuccotti Park that is located several blocks from Wall Street after police prevented their occupation of the real Wall Street. [x] Complaints from residents and businesses in the area started immediately. Incessant noise from drumming above legally permissible levels was a persistent gripe, although many other violations were documented, including illegal camping, rape, assaults on police officers, illegal sale and consumption of prohibited drugs and alcohol, public urination and defecation in and near the park, and generally unsanitary and unhealthy conditions that protesters prevented authorities from remedying.

In spite of ample evidence that city laws and the rules of the park were violated, city politicians and police refrained from enforcing the law for two months, hiding behind First Amendment rights to free speech and assembly, as if the First Amendment also conferred the right to break the law. Authorities were apparently cowed by the fact that overwhelming majorities of New York City residents were in favor of allowing the protesters to remain in Zuccotti, regardless of the law. So authorities chose to go with the mob rule version of democracy for the first two months. When the mayor and police finally did decide to remove the protesters, it was only after support for them in public opinion polls had declined significantly, perhaps to less than a majority. The appearance of a willingness to enforce the law only when a majority seems to be in favor of doing so, leaves citizens on both sides of the issues feeling the need to constantly defend their rights personally and, for that matter, to do as the Occupiers were doing, which is to look for opportunities to use the political process to take property from others.

"This is how democracy is supposed to work," President Obama told Steve Croft on 60 Minutes regarding the debate over raising taxes on the rich. "It's not because we're trying to punish the rich. I want everyone to be rich – that's great." [xi] Leaving aside the absurdity of rich being something everyone could be without destroying the meaning of the word, the President is certainly right as a political matter in today's America, which he and other Blue Team members present as a fight between 360,000 rich people and 160 million middle class people. President Obama's 60 Minutes interview, which followed his speech in Osawatomie, Kansas on December 6, 2011, drew heavily on former President Theodore Roosevelt's Osawatomie speech of August 31, 1910. In that earlier speech, Roosevelt endorsed the budding progressive movement in American politics, giving it a formal name more in character with his Rough Riders reputation: the "New Nationalism."

Whatever their labels, both presidents are miles from the original concepts of America's Founders, who knew that without a property-based notion of justice, there could be no peace between factions warring over property. The Founders would be aghast at the common Blue Team chant, No Justice, No Peace, since it turns on the exact opposite meaning of justice than the one they had in mind. The Founders would also have been aghast at President Roosevelt, who argued in Osawatomie that social justice was more important than property rights, as if these concepts were incompatible. He could easily have coined the No Justice, No Peace slogan, and certainly did what he could to promote it in principle, as has President Obama. Both presidents pushed with all their might to effect downward redistribution, considering it a moral obligation of government to counter inequality.

Because the Founders admired Adam Smith, they understood that inequality is an important source of incentives to work hard and invest, and thus has great value to an economy. Smith's *invisible hand* works largely on the basis of the incentives individuals have to improve their condition, which is a motive that both depends on and creates inequality. Moreover, the more inequality there is, the more powerful the incentive. The more you can divide, subdivide and name the various levels of income and wealth – in other words, the steeper the inequality gradient – the greater will be your desire to work hard. Even the much-maligned greed and envy, not to mention the fear of falling back down, can play useful roles energizing the economy by motivating people to continue to work as they move up the ladder.

But while fear, greed and envy are valuable when a society respects property, these same emotions work against a society that loses respect for property. Then they will cause factions to spring up and spend all their energies inciting the rage of mobs demanding other people's property. This is at best a zero-sum game for the mobs. But it is a bonanza for government, which will grow ever larger as it turns the top echelons of society into a complicit elite that assists authorities in their confiscate-and-redistribute game. The way the elite does this is by shaping politically correct arguments for popular policies, those thousand-and-one entitlements to other people's money that take form as proposals and then programs under their expert guidance.

The governing elite class extends far beyond the elected politicians, appointed bureaucrats and their staffs that make up the official government. The full elite also includes upper management at large corporations, union leaders, lobbyists, antitrust and patent lawyers, university academics, newspaper and television editors, op-ed writers, talking heads and all others with the expertise to help shape public attitudes toward the issues of the day, which inevitably benefit either the Red Team or the Blue Team in their redistribution contests. Even seemingly unrelated issues and activities are indirectly related to distribution because they help identify the character or positions of the debaters in ways that shape attitudes and votes. The bulk of everyone's attention is taken up by the effort, either to reshape the future distribution landscape through rules or politics, or to deal with the current configuration. Our best minds are thus engaged in the top-down reengineering of our society, re-jiggering the relationships between classes, age groups, sexes, races and all the other divisions of our people to suit the latest politically correct theories.

As the elites debate and deal in the minutiae of rules and policies that have redistribution effects, they are, for all practical purposes, engaged in governing. Like all governing elites, from kings and emperors on down, the modern elite has positions that are lucrative, inaccessible and secure, compared to the people they rule. While anyone can theoretically join the elite, loyalty to the class demands a degree of political correctness that rivals the imperial loyalties of old, and that not just anyone can master. These experts are all VIPs in the fast lane of life, creating power and wealth for themselves through their control of redistribution, lording it over average citizens who are frightened and shamed into supporting "the democratic process." *This is how democracy is supposed to work!* No justice, no peace, indeed.

3. Logical Conclusion

Occupy Wall Street protesters would be surprised to learn that the U. S. Securities & Exchange Commission got to their target first, and has already virtually destroyed Wall Street. The SEC's attack began seriously in the mid-1990s, [xii] promoting wealth-spreading reforms Occupy would approve of. Pushing fairness and level playing fields, the Commission aimed to redistribute income and advantage from big block traders to little individual investors. But in a magnificent example of the danger of unintended consequences, the Commission also wiped out the capital raising function of Wall Street along with the block traders. Since this function is considered to be Wall Street's raison d'être, its loss would be a net loss for investors and the economy, even if the attempted redistribution had actually occurred. But it didn't. All the little investors got was an electronic casino of hyper-fast trading that they abhor.

Trading costs are lower now than they were on the old Wall Street. But the negative surprises have long since overwhelmed any advantage in trading costs. In addition to the creation of high frequency trading and the destruction of IPOs, there is the loss of the millions of jobs that would have been created if IPOs had remained at pre-reform levels. [xiii] There is also the sharp decline in the number of listed stocks since the reforms began, as those that disappear through merger, bankruptcy and other events are not replaced due to the lack of IPOs. And then there is the increase in "black swan" volatility events, from the Flash Crash of 2010 to the BATS and Facebook IPOs and the Knightmare of 2012. Most troubling of all, the incomprehensible operating mechanics of today's market leave investors big and small feeling disadvantaged and gamed.

> Poll after poll shows that investors feel the markets are tilted unfairly against them. What's worse is that investor skepticism is higher than it was before "reforms" allegedly improved the system. [xiv]

It is clear now that even the staunchest believers in those automated trading reforms are beginning to abandon ship, embarrassed, perhaps, at what their advocacy has created:

> For several years, the Wall Street wizards who built a faster, more fragmented stock market justified their creation by pointing to the benefits it yielded for investors in the form of lower trading costs. But as the speed and complexity of the markets have continued to change at a rapid pace – with trade times now measured in millionths of a second – a growing number of studies and market participants suggest that those benefits to investors have stalled or even started to reverse. [xv]

One important difference between Occupy Wall Street protesters and the government regulators of Wall Street is that, while the former have understandable gripes due to a lack of jobs, the latter have the most secure jobs around on what is left of Wall Street. While bankers' and traders' jobs have been disappearing since the SEC's reforms began, the regulators that put them out of business have been growing in number and job security as they seized control of market structure. This fact can explain why, while the academics that once supported them in lockstep have begun to waver, there is no indication that any such self-doubt is emerging at the SEC. On the contrary, the arrogance and certainty that the Commission is and always has been right has only increased with growing evidence that it was and is wrong. This arrogance has even led to a plethora of new rules based on the same big-is-bad and spread-the-wealth theories that created the current problems, as the Large Trader rule, the Market Access rule, the Consolidated Audit Trail rule and other proposals circle the wagons around the SEC's automation mission.

To understand how we got here and where we are going, it is helpful to place this event in the context of similar ones that have occurred over the past century. From this perspective, the SEC's attack on Wall Street was just another sweep of a small-world network into government hands. Similar things had happened with oil, electric utilities, telephones, airlines, computers and many other industries. In all cases the government took over an industry that had been running efficiently in order to artificially insert competition into it.

The rationales for the takeovers were based primarily on antitrust and its wealth-spreading effects, and secondarily on its efficiency-enhancing effects. Ironically, and illustrating the theoretical confusion of antitrust, theorists are divided over whether antitrust has or should have any wealth-spreading goals or effects. In any case, the methods for addressing both inequality and inefficiency are the same: first, creating more competition by helping little guys compete with big guys at providing the industry's primary product and, second, helping consumers of that product by lowering its price through such competition. Because it envelops different, indeed often diametrically opposite and mutually incompatible underlying theories – such as the to-redistribute-or-not question – antitrust has achieved nearly universal academic and political support, and has built an ever-larger edifice on a foundation of sand. [xvi]

In spite of its soft foundation, antitrust gave an ever-expanding number of jobs to bureaucrats for the further design and management of network industries. In addition to regulators, there was plenty of wealth and power to go around for politicians and their cronies in industry, not to mention large numbers of supporting staff, such as their antitrust and intellectual property lawyers. Throw in the assorted academics, editors, pundits and others who weigh in on issues and rule filings, and a pretty clear picture emerges of what the governing elite looks like for these industries. But so confusing is antitrust that the public can't tell that all the debaters are really on the same side on the issue that matters most to these elites, namely that of their own importance. Both the Red Team and the Blue Team start their arguments by bowing to the government and declaring their allegiance to it. The obsequiousness with which they approach the antitrust process implicitly acknowledges the legitimacy of its power to redistribute, and serves to emphasize the importance of their own role in the process.

In network science jargon, all of these government takeovers replace *aristocratic* small worlds with *egalitarian* or *random* small worlds. Rather than allowing the hubs that rose to dominance through *rich get richer* or *preferential attachment* to continue growing, government instead restrains or reverses their dominance based on spread-the-wealth principles. Whether it is called antitrust, deregulation or network neutrality, or rides in on less formal terms, like fairness, competition, transparency or efficiency, such government action always has the effect of encouraging the creation of more nodes and direct connections between the nodes, rather than relying on super-connecting hubs acting as intermediaries.

All of the industries that were subject to such takeovers have been riddled with disappointments and unintended consequences. Analyses of what went wrong, however, have been less than enlightening, because they have been distorted by the overwhelming presence of redistribution in the arguments and tend, therefore, to be self-justifying no matter how dysfunctional the industry becomes. More competition, for example, is always commended, no matter how unattractive the product becomes, because competition is expected to aid redistribution through lower prices. Cheap long distance rates and airline tickets are assumed to trump complaints over incomprehensible phone bills and a miserable flying experience, while the consumer frustrated over bad and unresponsive service is ignored.

The dogged determination of the elite to apply competition theory to industries that are sickened by previous applications of the same theory is reminiscent of how physicians once applied bloodletting to every malady known to man, upping the dose until the patient either died from loss of blood or, miraculously, recovered. That some patients recovered in spite of the treatment does not mean they benefitted from the often-massive loss of blood. The fact that industries that have been busted by antitrust still muddle along at low levels of satisfaction is not evidence that competition policy has benefitted them, or that more of it will benefit them even more. It is evidence of a sickness on the part of the physician.

That is why a new perspective is in order, one that network scientists are in a unique position to provide. Some of them are beginning to wonder if overall network efficiency suffers without the coordinating effect of preferential attachment resulting in hubs. If so, then the switch from aristocratic to egalitarian networks may be the reason that capacity constraints, logjams and bottlenecks are appearing in airlines, electric utilities and other "deregulated" industries into which artificial competition has been inserted. [xvii] The stock market may provide the best opportunity yet for a case study of this problem from a network science perspective.

On the old Wall Street, both the NYSE and Nasdaq served the function of super-connectors or hubs. Each operated in separate, though highly related, spheres of activity. Everyone interested in trading seasoned stocks came to the NYSE. Everyone interesting in trading new stocks or buying IPOs came to Nasdaq. These were separate functions, with separate lists of stocks and different market structures. The separations by function, trading structure and list provided firm anchoring points to which chains of likewise differentiated intermediaries were attached. Each broker and dealer was likely to have separate "OTC" and "listed" desks serving Nasdaq and NYSE interests, respectively.

It is difficult to overstate the degree of specialization that such differentiation encouraged and the complexity of the ecosystems that grew up around these different but very related activities. The participants became very familiar with their roles through the evolution of their daily habits, which centered on personal interaction governed by a Dictum Meum Pactum ethical system: My word is my bond. [xviii] This in turn allowed the overall ecosystems to fulfill their capital formation, price discovery and liquidity functions in a reliable and expanding fashion that supported robust job growth and economic vitality.

Under the SEC's reforms, differentiation disappeared and the ecosystems dried up. Now exchanges and exchange-like systems are being created at a breakneck pace, including several that are sponsored by each of the NYSE and Nasdaq. A couple of newcomer exchanges have joined the fray, too, each of which also sponsors several entries in the race. Instead of one exchange for each stock, now there are over 50 exchanges and exchange-like entities competing with those old monopolies. The net effect is that the hubs, as intended, have been destroyed. The original monopoly exchanges have disintegrated under the proliferating fragmentation as their market shares collapsed to less than 25% from over 80%. With the rules emphasizing fast connections between all of these new and old exchanges and systems, as if they were undifferentiated nodes on a network, they are all becoming just that. Differentiation and specialization are out. Low latency is in.

Not surprisingly after such a radical change, the markets seem to have also changed in terms of their ability to fulfill their traditional functions. They no longer are able to reliably support capital formation, price discovery, liquidity provision, job growth or economic vitality, all of which have languished since the SEC's reforms. According to Congressman Darrell Issa, the U.S. IPO market is now closed to 80% of the companies that need an IPO, and the U.S. share of the value of international IPOs dropped from 77.3% in 1996 to 13.8% in 2007 and to 1.9% in 2008. [xix] As to the market's inability to reliably support price discovery and liquidity provision, their sudden disappearance in the Flash Crash on May 6, 2010 is the most eloquent witness so far, an event that had no remotely comparable precedent before the SEC's reforms. [xx] To get a handle on why such problems might have occurred, and in particular why they are explainable from the perspective of disturbances to the stock market as a network, we need to look at how the changes can be expressed as changes in nodes and links and how these have changed the character of stock market networks.

The old market-making system built around block trading was one of those chains connected to the NYSE and Nasdaq. As such, it was also specialized by function and list. When considering which traders to deal with – i.e., which nodes to connect to – a given block trader would consider such things as a potential counterparty's reputation, size and the number of trusting counterparties the other trader dealt with. Such subjective factors to determine the *fitness* [xxi] of potential counterparties drove a classic case of preferential attachment, leading to the rich getting richer, as the well-connected got even better connected. Block trading was the ultimate aristocratic network.

The SEC's reforms wiped out the block-trading structure and its ecosystem. It is being replaced by high frequency trading, which is much less aristocratic and much more random or egalitarian in form. This was to be expected, because preferential attachment may not be able to operate under anonymous trading, which the electronic reforms virtually required. It is hard to vet a potential counterparty's fitness if you don't know who he is.

The reforms' signature requirement was to force attachment to many nodes whether attachment was preferred or not, by mandating that "best price" must be accessed. The automatic accessing of the best price available at the time an order enters any one of the many markets in the National Market System has been the core principle underlying NMS since it was first conceived, and is formalized in a legal obligation of brokers and exchanges to provide "best execution." The fear was that, if the markets were not electronically and transparently connected by rule, trades would occur at prices that were inferior to those that could be gotten with the connections. No consideration was given to the possibility that investors might prefer to choose their own markets based on those markets' ability to give them what they actually wanted, rather than what regulators said they should want. Accordingly it was mandated that the "best" treatment would be required to occur no matter which market an investor entered the NMS through, by routing and rerouting an order around until it found the best price. Mandating best price or best execution is the key legal means by which this regulatory goal was accomplished.

Regulation NMS, implemented in 2007, is the latest and most draconian version of the best price rule, because it applied to all stocks, even those on the NYSE, which had previously escaped its purview, and because it required all the routing and rerouting to be done immediately. Because high frequency traders (HFTs), exchanges and other participants are now required by Reg. NMS to be connected directly or indirectly to any possible source of best price, the number of competitors has exploded, which of course was the purpose of the policy in the first place. And because the reforms mandated that the accessing of best price must be immediate, they put a premium not only on getting connected to them all, but on getting connected directly to them rather than indirectly through hubs or other intermediaries. Once the direct connection hint took hold, competition took over so that now all serious competitors have direct connections to many of their significant counterparties.

These changes have not been analyzed yet from a network science perspective. Among the interesting features to explore is the new network's focus on speed, not just on connections per se. Six degrees wouldn't cut it, if it requires extra time to get to that other person through all the intermediate handshakes. This need for speed and direct connections has led to breathtaking advances in technology. Since the number of nodes has been virtually mandated to keep increasing via competition policies like best price, the technical requirements are daunting and perhaps unprecedented in network lore. Imagine if traders were directly connected to each other (one degree of separation) and could send each other messages in one one-thousandth of a second, and for some reason some traders sometimes sent hundreds of messages per second to some other traders. And then imagine that all the messages in the system had to be recorded and immediately disseminated to all people on a "tape." And then imagine that such blindingly fast transparency encouraged the multiplication of quotes per trade into the tens, then hundreds, then thousands, particularly in the case of options, [xxii] and that all of those quote messages also had to be disseminated. Such a system is the logical conclusion of all the SEC's National Market System policies and, believe it or not, we're already there.

So fundamental is HFTs' need for speed that they virtually require co-location of their order generating processes at exchanges and other liquidity sources. Even at the speed of light, miles, feet and maybe even millimeters matter.

The speed that HFTs require creates in turn a desperate need for speed on the part of exchanges. Any exchange that fails to attract HFTs will die for lack of liquidity. And any HFT that waits around on slow exchanges will die, too, as competitors get to all the good trades first. So the exchanges have no choice but to chase low latency as fast as they can.

The consequence of this is that the small-world efficiency that brought everyone together at an understandable pace on the old Wall Street has been replaced by rapid fire quoting and trading as all the data makes its way through all the nodes, which are making this task ever more difficult because the nodes themselves are exploding in number under the policy. Trading-related message rates have exceeded six million per second, [xxiii] up from negligible before the government takeover began in 1997, and the rate appears set to continue doubling every year or two. Apparently, *positive feedback*, a phenomenon often associated in network science with network formation, is pushing this time toward network destruction.

Many remember the positive feedback that caused the Crash of October 19, 1987. In short, portfolio insurance caused sell orders that pushed the market down, which triggered more sell orders that pushed it down further, which triggered more sell orders that pushed it down further, etc. Something like that is happening again now. But this time, it is happening not to market prices, but to the market structure itself. Of course, if the structure is disrupted enough, that could eventually affect prices, too. And there have already been harbingers of what that might look like, such as the Flash Crash of May 6, 2010.

Because of their need to attract HFTs, the race for low latency and increased capacity is a critical business requirement of every stock exchange today. What goes generally unrecognized, however, is that the success of individual exchanges in this endeavor is counterproductive to the efficiency and stability of the overall industry network within which they all operate. More speed and more data spewing from any particular node, while necessary for that node's commercial survival, can only increase the difficulty that other nodes and the overall network experience in handling the greater and faster data flows emanating from that successful node.

What is also missed is how these elements play off against each other to produce even greater positive feedback. For example, success at any one exchange to lower latency, i.e., to increase the speed at which each quote or print is processed, challenges all the other exchanges and the overall market to create more capacity to handle the larger number of quotes and prints coming from that particular node. And the more any or all of them are successful at lowering latency, the bigger the data processing challenges they throw out to all the other nodes and the whole market. Even within each exchange, the more capacity it has to process numbers of quotes and prints, the greater its need for speed in handling each one, and vice versa. So increases in speed drive an exchange toward increasing its capacity, and increases in capacity drive an exchange toward increasing its speed. And successes on both of these fronts multiply the problems that other exchanges and the whole system experience in processing the overall market's trading needs.

Speed and capacity aren't the only contributors to this positive feedback loop. There are dozens of other elements that similarly feed back into the National Market System and exacerbate its data processing challenges. All of them are either explicit SEC policies or indirect consequences of those policies. For example:

- Competition policies fragment markets and multiply the number of nodes (exchanges, ATSs, ECNs, dark pools and other stock trading systems, as well as mandatory data dissemination systems and regulatory oversight systems) that need to be connected and whose activity must be dealt with under best execution and data dissemination rules;
- Declining trade size has become the norm, as algorithms are used to hide large orders from transparency by shredding them into many tiny pieces and randomizing their times and places of entry into the market while using as many nodes as possible to confuse participants;
- Since algorithms hide large orders primarily by shredding them among multiple nodes, the more nodes there are, the more algorithms are necessary, and the more algorithms there are, the more nodes will be sought and accommodated;
- Algorithmic trading, which is effectively required by the fact of automated trading in a fragmented multi-node marketplace, is much faster, in fact thousands or millions of times faster, in its order generating potential than human trading;
- Competition among algorithm providers and users pushes toward ever faster order generation by each algorithm;
- Transparency policies discourage the efficient matching of orders in dark environments that do not suffer the data and coordination challenges required of matching in lit markets;
- Anonymous trading, which discourages reputation-based handling of large orders, has taken over most trading, so fewer large orders are being matched as blocks, which forces increases in the number of quotes and trades needed to handle the same volume of shares;
- Transparency, anonymity, and high-frequency trading in general, which combined to remove human negotiation of trades, have caused exponential increases in the number of quotes and quote changes needed to execute a trade;
- The more quotes and trades needed to handle the same volume of shares, the faster trading has to go to process them all, and because of the positive feedback in the factors listed above, the faster trading

goes at any given moment, the faster it will be forced to go in the future.

Summing up: the volume of trading related messages is increasing dramatically, required to do so by such factors as the declining trade size due to larger trades being broken up, the increase in the number of quotes per trade, the increase in the number of nodes in the overall market, the greater speed and capacity of each node, each algorithm, each matching engine, each tape and quote delivery system and many other factors. Similar problems are arising in other countries where regulators follow the SEC's lead, such as in the United Kingdom, Europe, Canada and India. For example:

- Inter-market linkage and passporting policies, like NMS in the US and MiFID [xxiv] in Europe, increase the number of markets that must be taken account of when trading, i.e., the number of nodes;
- Best price routing rules or equivalent implied fiduciary obligations confer standing on marginal markets, including both old regional ones linked or passported in, and newly created ones;
- Aggressive transparency rules, like Canada's trade-at rule, similar to a proposed U.S. rule, make efficient block matching unable to provide relief to the high-frequency frenzy; [xxv]
- The market shares of all of the major stock markets of the West are collapsing under these fragmenting antitrust policies, which are ongoing and accelerating;
- Markets all over the world whose regulators are following the SEC's lead in imposing electronic competition are beginning to experience their own snafus, too, and are desperately trying to install their own circuit breakers to contain them as the most bizarre price movements traders have ever seen are described by officials as occurring when their systems are functioning normally. [xxvi]

As troubling as these developments already are from a network coordination perspective, they are likely to get much worse, for two reasons. First, regulators are pushing for authority to include other markets than stock markets under their transparent electronic regimes, such as fixed income, currencies and OTC derivatives. And second, regulators are pushing to make all stock markets global, which could force the linking of them all. This would not, as it might first sound, lead to a consolidation of systems. Rather, since antitrust is an inherently fragmenting force, the linking would further empower the fragmentation, and increase, not decrease, the number of nodes, as well as enhance the urgent need for speedy, direct connections between all of them.

If regulators follow their competition theories to their logical conclusion, international mergers of whole marketplaces could occur, thereby quickly exploding the number of nodes and ratcheting up the challenges described above by an order of magnitude or two. Major exchange groups would encourage this result, since the largest already own multiple markets spanning several national jurisdictions. And regulators are already coining licenses of various kinds at the drop of a hat, including multiple authorizations for each of the four major exchanges in the United States. It would thus seem peculiar to resist requests by exchanges to also list foreign markets' stocks, just as most of the competitors list each other's domestic stocks now under their "unlisted trading privileges," or UTP. Indeed, it would be inconsistent with the regulatory principles driving this frenzy not to acquiesce to the full international passporting of all markets.

A globally linked market of markets, a Global Market System (GMS), will likely be hailed with all the fanfare that the antitrust breakup of the national champions was greeted, such as when the SEC launched its National Market System attack on the NYSE and Nasdaq. Nations that resist connection to the GMS machine may prove to be useful control cases to assess what helps and what hurts a capital formation network and a nation's economy. Resisters so far in Turkey, Brazil and China look like the odds-on favorites [xxvii] to lead the next phase of capitalism while the grand old markets of the West drink the competition Kool-Aid together.

Such developments can be looked at as errors in market structure. But the more interesting approach now is to look at market structure itself from the perspective of network formation and destruction. Network scientists have grappled with what makes networks robust and what makes them weak, what makes them grow and come together, and what makes them disintegrate. They have done this in the interest of defending natural ecosystem networks from collapse due to human activity, and in the interest of destroying networks that are bad for humans, like viruses and terrorists. They have tested and discarded theories on what makes the Internet robust and what makes it vulnerable.

The Internet began, according to lore, with a plan to make critical United States' communications safe from accidental failure or enemy attack. [xxviii] Theorists thought a distributed approach would be better for this purpose and came up with the Internet. The idea was that any random harm to nodes and links in the redundant, distributed architecture would not be able to bring the Internet down. That may have been true when the Internet's design was still subject to human control. But once it got growing on its own under preferential attachment, the Internet didn't look as redundant and invulnerable as originally envisioned. While it had lots of nodes and links, the overwhelming majority of which were bit players and therefore unlikely to be fatal to the overall Internet if removed in random failures, the flip side of preferential attachment is that a power law also created hubs. What if there were attacks that deliberately targeted hubs? Scientists now aren't so sure the Internet is as invulnerable as they once thought it was.

Americans would be outraged if they thought what happened to our stock market were the work of al Qaeda or Chinese hackers. But the fact is that destroying stock market hubs was and is a deliberate policy of our government. The policy was carried out in the interest of confused goals like transparency, competition and a level playing field. As anyone who has ever bought or sold a house knows, it is a foolish strategy to transparently tell the other side your ultimate price. The SEC has turned that foolish strategy into a universal policy. Similarly, as anyone who has ever sold a painting at auction knows, getting everyone into the auction house is the key to getting a good price. Having dozens of competing auction houses will only dilute the competition for your painting and confuse bidders. Ordinary people pursuing ordinary ends, like buying houses or selling paintings, can see these things. It is only the experts at the SEC that cannot.

The level playing field, too, is a thoroughly inappropriate goal of regulation. As I described in a 1997 letter to the SEC, treating trading as a sporting event can only destroy the potential for more fit market structures to evolve. Indeed, requiring fairness, as if trading were a sporting event, will destroy the efficient structures that have already evolved, such as the NYSE's auction market and Nasdaq's dealer market.

> Darwinian competition . . . discovers which new forms of competitors are better at surviving than old forms . . . Because their struggle for survival is between different forms of competitors, it is inherently unfair by the terms of sports competition. But, far from hindering the effectiveness of evolution, this unfairness is essential to producing ever more capable competitors and ever more complex forms of biological, social and economic organization. In a very real sense, Darwinian competition must be unfair to work properly. [xxix]

The NYSE and Nasdaq dominated their niches because their structures had proved very effective at such tasks as discovering price and raising capital. It is almost certainly no coincidence that they have lost those talents since the SEC upended their structures. One needn't be versed in evolution theory, market structure theory, or any other science or theory to suspect this connection. Merely noting that flash crashes and IPO debacles never used to happen before the SEC changed things should be sufficient to reach this logical conclusion. Such black swan events should occur only every million or billion or trillion years or so. That they are happening several times a year now is a sign the SEC must have done something wrong. Again, ordinary people can see these things. But for some reason the SEC's experts can't.

Or can they? It certainly seems more likely by now that the errors of the SEC are too numerous and egregious for even the self-interested Commission to ignore. As I described in *War on Wealth,* the Commission's interest is in forcing change on the market, whether or not the change does any good. [xxx] It is obviously not in the Commission's interest to admit the emperor has no clothes, to admit that it can also see the things any ordinary citizen not in the grip of politically correct excuses for Commission errors can see. The lack of candor at the SEC would be funny if it weren't so serious. Here we have the agency officially in charge of keeping Americans fraud free and honest perpetrating fraud upon fraud upon the people it is supposed to protect from dishonesty, telling lie after lie about the debacles its reforms have caused.

Network scientists might be able to help. For example, they could explain what happens to networks when their hubs are removed. Can they survive? If not, can you make them re-grow? If not, can you let them re-grow naturally so they will do again what they used to do? If not, can government make people do what the networks used to do, but without a network this time? The answer to all of these questions appears to be no. We are therefore in a real policy pickle when it comes to capital markets. It takes the natural operation of preferential attachment to create robust networks, but the form they take from there is anybody's guess. This means that forcing networks to do what we want them to through human policy is not possible. Destroying them, however, is easy.

4. Connecting the Dots

Mathematicians know network science as "graph theory." This convention emerged as some famous mathematical problems boiled down to discovering rules for connecting dots on paper. They were not really graphs, such as with X and Y axes, but conceptual illustrations on which to present problems and propose solutions. A famous early one puzzled over how to walk over all seven bridges near a well-known mathematician's town without crossing any bridge twice. [xxxi] A modern puzzle that feels similar connects all nine dots on a three by three grid using only four straight lines without lifting the pencil or going backwards. The solution to this one gave us the famous "outside the box" phrase.

Apart from puzzle enthusiasts and mathematicians, graphs had little practical relevance until they were used to illustrate real networks, such as telephones, the Internet and the World Wide Web. This expanded opportunities both for describing the observed world mathematically and for empirically testing mathematical theories.

Advances quickened in the 1990s when scientists focused in on networks not so much as fixed structures, but as evidence of a process of formation, a coming together of order out of chaos driven by network effects. Understanding these dynamic forces involved thinking through not only how pre-existing dots on a graph linked up with each other, but what happened when placing new dots on the graphs or, more generally, during the ongoing birth and death of all the new and old nodes and links. Contemplating these matters led to the most important breakthrough in modern network science, namely that nodes tend to link to other nodes with more connections rather than to nodes with fewer connections. This gave birth to the concept of preferential attachment, or rich get richer, which turned out to be the key to understanding self-organization, emergence, complexity, fractals, phase transitions and many other strange creatures dotting the network science landscape. True to its name, rich get richer was indeed what created all those inequality monsters since Pareto's peapods. [xxxii]

With such anthropomorphic characterizations, it was perhaps inevitable that moral judgments would eventually enter the picture. As if preferential attachment and rich get richer weren't target enough, scientists came up with one tainted term after another to describe the unfair, biased, discriminatory and callous way that nature operates. In the field of industrial organization, *tipping points* led to *lock-in* of inferior technologies, granting monopolies to those who by luck or nefarious means gained a *first mover advantage*. This was welcome news to trustbusters. With the new science in hand as a roadmap, regulators broke up monopolies that were violating antitrust, or otherwise forced them to succumb to regulatory guidance. The cases against Microsoft and Intel were the most visible, but there were many others. In fact it is fair to say that network science became the deus ex machina that rescued antitrust from its own inconsistencies and theoretical flaws.

Robert H. Bork's 1978 classic, *The Antitrust Paradox: A Policy at War with Itself* articulates the traditional problems of antitrust in a work that arrived well before the network effect revolution. In *Paradox,* Bork seemed ambivalent as to whether antitrust was worth keeping, or should be scrapped for incorrect and inconsistent interpretations of Congressional intent and consequent vagueness. In the end, Bork came down on the side of keeping antitrust, perhaps because, as he noted with seeming nostalgia, it was "a law that became, and for a long time remained, the politically potent symbol of the virtues of free and unregulated markets." [xxxiii] But although there has been plenty of time to address at least some of the antitrust flaws Bork and others have pointed out over the years, there is little evidence that any of them have been addressed.

But then along came network science in the 1990s with its new angle on old violations. The Justice Department's Antitrust Division was a quick study of the new theories. So were the FTC, the FCC and the SEC. All of them glommed on in particular to the tainted terms mentioned above: tipping points, lock-in, first-mover-advantage. Justice moved on Microsoft with a vengeance, its former head Joel Klein hiring star attorney David Boies to nail Bill Gates for his aggressive tactics. With the new theories in hand, it was suddenly easy to explain to the court why monopolists do what they do and why, therefore, it was necessary to block them or break up the results of their work.

A few network scientists offered their assistance. Mathematicians with a knack for explaining complex theories, like Brian Arthur, told the pioneering trustbusters how "increasing returns," positive feedback and lock-in would indeed lead to monopolies of inferior technologies blocking better ones, monopolies that would not necessarily dissolve under natural competition, as previous free market advocates had asserted they would. [xxxiv] Instead, the scientists said, regulation, i.e., antitrust, was needed to prevent such monopolies from gaining unfair advantage, and particularly from blocking new technologies through lock-in. [xxxv]

Such arguments were music to the ears of trustbusters, suddenly giving them the scientific legitimacy to cut through all the carping from Bork and others. It became fashionable to say that network effects were particularly evident in the new technology industries, especially computers, computer software and telecommunications. This gave both the bureaucrats and their scientific advisors a new sense of their own importance, since the logic of their story is that, if we don't get the law right, and soon, then all progress will grind to a lock-in halt. Other critical industries, including some very old ones, were also targeted for attack. In the stock market, network effect theory added fresh momentum to the ongoing moves to bust NYSE and Nasdaq with multiple market competition, an effort that had been building since the National Market System was launched in 1975. [xxxvi]

In response to these attacks, accused monopolists have foolishly continued the "denial defense" strategy I described in *Countdown.* [xxxvii] Under this strategy, the accused contend that competition naturally takes care of monopolies, implying that they wouldn't have bothered with monopolization since it wouldn't work anyway. Unfortunately for them, competition doesn't naturally take care of monopolies, at least not in the single silo of competition that antitrust posits as the relevant field. We'll come back shortly to why this antitrust single-silo construct is an inappropriately constrained view of competition. But first we need to acknowledge that, if that inappropriate view is taken, then indeed the trustbusters and their scientific advisors are right. The denial defense collapses under the rapidly accumulating evidence that lock-in does happen, monopolization can work, and monopolies can exist at least for a while without being undone by competition. As a result of following their denial defense strategies, the accused monopolists were caught red-handed, but stubbornly stuck to stories that can now easily be shown to be incorrect theoretically. Moreover, given that the monopolists were in network businesses, they must have known that the theories they were propounding didn't hold water and, therefore, that their claims of innocence were disingenuous. It was this evident disingenuousness that enabled David Boies to pillory Bill Gates, the event that led to the collapse of Microsoft's and Intel's runs in the stock market and, not coincidentally, the beginning of the end of America's technology leadership in the world.

A new angle on network research is needed. The traditional focus on networks as discrete, single fields is both an antitrust policy preference and a virtual patent policy requirement. Both of these bodies of law seek to constrain networks within narrow channels of limited value and duration that can be legally controlled or extinguished by regulators. But this is not how nature works, nor does it provide a framework for the natural path of scientific inquiry. From a network research standpoint, while it may be easier to think of the World Wide Web and the Internet as separate networks, they are obviously highly entangled. So too are all the telecommunications networks, the computer networks, the computer software networks, the social gaming networks, the social networks, the church networks, the community organization networks, the business organization networks, the education networks, the political networks, the stock market networks and virtually every network you can name. None exists separately and independently of its environment any more than the lion or the cactus exist outside of the jungle or the desert. And even the jungle and the desert overlap in places, as well as give each other wide berth in others. Like species, networks form largely in relation to other networks, sometimes sidling up and free riding on an ecological neighbor's success, and sometimes separating from it in order to avoid challenging a winner.

Both sidling up and separating are antitrust violations, called *tying* and *market division*, respectively. Trustbusters endlessly busy themselves determining when firms like Microsoft have gotten too close to a neighboring market by tying their market power in one field, like computer operating systems and software applications, to another they'd like to enter, like Web browsing. As to separating, the same trustbusters wring their hands over firms that engage in market division to avoid competing with a winner in another niche, like Microsoft and Intel did as the Wintel duo, or as the NYSE and Nasdaq did with their distinctly separate lists of stocks and different market structures.

We know what happened to Microsoft and Intel. Less well known is that both NYSE and Nasdaq were busted in essence not for market division, per se, (although market division is a "per se" violation, i.e., one of the most egregious kind, for which there is theoretically no defense), but for being too distinct. NYSE was not multi-dealer like Nasdaq was, and Nasdaq was not multi-market (best-price) like NYSE's auction was. In separate regulatory channels over the years, the SEC gradually forced rules on each market that had the ancillary effect of outlawing the other's market structure. [xxxviii] Being too distinct is not an official antitrust violation of any kind, much less a per se violation (although, as said above, market division is). But in further evidence of the theoretical inconsistency and confusion of antitrust, the Commission applied the "fair competition" concept in such a way that both the NYSE and Nasdaq came to be judged against the rules that had been developed for the other. The result was that both were forced to look like each other, as the SEC "auctionized" the dealer market and "dealerized" the auction market. [xxxix] In the end both became nearly identical electronic systems as they were forced to abandon the distinct structures that had made them successful in their different niches.

Viewing networks and industries only as separate and discrete entities not only leads to bad policy, but it leads to bad science, or at least incomplete science. When research mirrors regulators' discrete-network-by-discrete-network approach, that helps regulators build their empires because it gives credence to their view that the world can be improved by separately defining and perfecting each network, as if it operated in total isolation from the world around it. But looking only at each network in isolation works against a clear understanding of how networks naturally form and what the overall import of network formation is. This is not how nature operates, or at least how it would operate if unmolested by policies devoted to preserving the power of regulators.

The Austrian philosophers Friedrich A. Hayek and Joseph A. Schumpeter may provide useful frameworks for the broader, all-inclusive analyses that are needed. Hayek, for example, used the term *catallaxy* to encompass the coordinating mass of separately identifiable economies that worked together in an economic environment. [xl] And Schumpeter's term *creative destruction* presents the dynamic turnover of monopolies as a constantly moving process of formation and destruction in which new, more fit networks replace older ones. [xli] It is pointless to worry about the lock-in of each minor, most-narrowly defined network, when no sooner has lock-in occurred, but forces both inside and outside the locked in technology's field are vying to leverage its temporary hold to their advantage, or to overthrow it. The advantage is usually soon eclipsed in the melee as some other field's lock-in advantage emerges with more appeal to ever-changing consumer tastes or a wider sweep of control than the first. Witness the changes in dominant locked in technologies as the focus moved from big computers to small ones, to software, to laptops, to tablets, to smart phones, to clouds, to social networks, to games, with the whole pot stirred all along by the Internet, etc. It is absurd to worry about the lock-in of any particular technology at any point in this progression, because it will inevitably be knocked hither and yon by forces both from within and from outside of its field, especially as the fields themselves are constantly narrowing or widening or combining or separating or, lest we forget, disappearing.

In different but related ways, both patent and antitrust laws authorize the governing elite to squelch some monopolies and encourage others, to take monopolies from some people and bestow them on others. The premise is that bureaucrats and judges can figure out, by following conflicting and ever-changing laws and rules, where good monopolies should be allowed and where bad monopolies should be taken away and killed or redistributed to others or run by government regulators. While the theory is that the authorities can incentivize the right people, like inventors, and dis-incentivize the bad people, like monopolizing monopolists, it is heroic to imagine that mere humans can do such a task effectively. If they could, then one would also have to conclude that nature, God and, for good measure, Darwin, were wrong. Whatever one believes about the capability of men to take over evolution or to eugenically rework the natural order, it is certain that even attempting to do so is a huge task, one that has granted its overseers dominant positions of power in our society. If one were honest, one would have to admit that those dominant overseers have made a mess of things.

To counter the overseers' hubris, scientists might start by looking for power laws and other network formation markers wherever they can find them. The obvious known or suspected networks should be examined for cross-network effects as network formation is enhanced or undermined through interaction with the environment, including both other networks and regulation. Look for signs that robust network formation has been enhanced or disrupted by regulation. And look for signs that regulation has created its own networks, and whether there is a correlation, positive or negative, between the robustness of regulatory enterprises as networks and the robustness of the industries administered by regulators – again, as networks. Examining the growth of the governing elite class as a network may be particularly fruitful. It might even be fun to look for various versions of the *Kevin Bacon game* playing out in crony capitalism connections. [xlii]

It would be interesting to contrast in terms of network robustness the growth of the governing elite class with the decline of the networks that that class oversees. Examples of places to look for evidence would include:

- The growth in personnel at the SEC and other antitrust agencies;
- The growth in their senior regulators' compensation, including pension and deferred compensation arrangements as well as the value of revolving door opportunities;
- The growth in their job security versus industry job security;
- The growth in the number of pages in the Federal Register devoted to stock market rules;
- The growth in the number of comment letters;
- The growth in the number of and connections among footnotes in rule proposals in the Federal Register and in comment letters on those proposals, as well as in concept releases and other regulatory releases;
- The growth in stock market fragmentation as measured by the number of competitors;
- The growth in the number of antitrust lawyers;
- The growth in the number of patent lawyers and of patent filings and actions;
- The growth in the number of patent and antitrust cases and regulatory actions and the time and pages devoted to them;
- The growth in time and money devoted to regulatory compliance.

The governing elite class may have spawned some of the strongest networks around on the strength of its evident twin missions: #1 – to grow itself at all costs, and #2 – to destroy all other competing networks by dismantling or killing them under antitrust and patent laws.

Mussolini, it is said, made the trains run on time. Whether or not this is true (and a quick search of the phrase will find many who dispute it), the belief is common that government is needed to create a certain minimal amount of order so that free markets can thrive, and the myth of Mussolini making the trains run on time is frequently trotted out in defense of that view. Another common myth trotted out for the same purpose is the need for government to create traffic laws or property laws, without which the basic organization of society would not exist and therefore commerce and other human interactions would be chaotic. This is all nonsense, as any network scientist can easily demonstrate.

The very nature of network formation is to bring order out of chaos. If natural network formation were allowed, not only would trains run on time and traffic run smoothly, but all of the other potential sources of conflict between humans over property and other issues would be resolved through superior organization to that which government overseers in their hubris can provide. It is simply not true that even free societies need a little bit of fascism to make the basics work. The basics and everything else will work much better under pure liberty. And it is precisely the need for organization that makes this so.

Railroad networks had been taken over by governments around the world long before Mussolini arrived on the scene. That Mussolini was able to improve things and "make the trains run on time" (or so his propagandists said) is not surprising. But that was only compared to the government-run mess that preexisted his arrival. The chaos that pertained before he came to power, as well as the chaos that his administration and Hitler's became the apotheosis of, had been artificially induced in the first place by the misplaced reliance on government to produce order. Had rail and other networks been allowed to continue to form naturally, not only would the trains have run on time all along, but humanity might have been spared the true chaos of the fascist and Nazi era. A commitment to allow natural network formation requires a prior commitment to protect an unalienable right to the pursuit of happiness. A people protected under such rights would not give a Mussolini or a Hitler the time of day.

In the aftermath of 9/11, our failure to "connect the dots" was posited as a reason the attacks occurred. [xliii] But the real danger may be our inability to make the connection between American policy and the chaos that has materialized under it. Naturally formed networks are the visible evidence that network effects have created order out of chaos. We should consider the possibility, therefore, that the dysfunctional industries that are emerging wherever we apply antitrust are becoming dysfunctional because of antitrust, the purpose of which is to break up networks. We may even find if we look carefully that terrorism itself is a threat we are creating with our policies to counter it.

5. Patent Falsehoods

The essential feature of natural law is that it is not arbitrary. It is simple and easy to understand. We know what it is and what our rights and obligations under it are. As long as we abide by it ourselves, natural law protects our life, liberty, goods and possessions from being taken by other people or government. This is not what the law looks like today in any country of the West, including the United States. The regulation of monopolies under antitrust and patent laws, in particular, is a sea of uncertainty. In fact, confusion reigns. And in confusion lurks an arbitrary government every bit as tyrannical as the English monarchy from which Americans fought a revolution to separate.

Some of the most valuable real estate in America has legal roots in patents granted by the kings of England through their representatives in the colonies, such as New York and New Jersey. They bear the names of prominent settlers, Indian tribes, physical landmarks or towns: The Claes Jansen Patent, The Tappan Patent, The Kakiat Patent, The Wawayanda Patent, The Orangetown Patent, The Stony Point Patent, The Lockhart Patent.

> In 1671, April 16, [Claes Jansen] obtained from the Duke of York [the king's brother], to whom Charles II had given proprietorship of this with other provinces, a tract of land 'lying on the Hudson River at the north end of Tappan, at a brook, thence northeasterly along the river 40 chains, thence northwesterly 60 chains to the foot of the mountains, thence south, southwest above the mountains 40 chains, thence south, southeast to the river at the point of the beginning, containing 240 acres.' [xliv]

Over time as patents for property in land became patents for property in inventions or "intellectual property," it became less clear where the boundaries were. A significant point on this path was the Copyright Clause, Article 1, Section 8, Clause 8 of the U.S. Constitution, which gave Congress the power to grant copyrights and patents:

> To promote the Progress of Science and useful Arts, by securing for limited Times to Authors and Inventors the exclusive Right to their respective Writings and Discoveries. [Federal Convention of 1787]

This is the language that led to the establishment of the United States Patent and Trademark Office, the USPTO. An important point must be noted in terms of what the Framers intended this provision to cover: "'useful Arts' does not refer to artistic endeavors, but rather to the work of artisans, people skilled in a manufacturing craft." [xlv] The language was thus intended to provide a regime for encouraging not only those quick sparks of genius associated with invention or writing, but also skills honed over time that improve manufacturing. This carried on the tradition of monopolies under which monarchs granted a wide variety of "sole seller" privileges, which is where the word, "monopoly" came from. [xlvi] Whatever was originally expected or intended, the monopoly oversight process spawned a vast bureaucracy including both intellectual property and antitrust, which because of its current arbitrariness is not consistent with natural law now.

From the standpoint of arbitrariness, patents stand out. Few inventors and no ordinary citizens can tell if an application is worth the time or money. The level of specialized expertise required to make such determinations is seldom available at any price, although patent lawyers will always be happy to charge for the time they spend trying to come up with an answer. Said answer will, however, as often as not be wrong. Partly this is due to the complexity of the field, which multiplies yearly. Partly it is due to changes in received wisdom that regularly shake things up, such as when "business process patents" are allowed and then disallowed and then allowed if they can be embodied in a physical machine, and then probably but not certainly disallowed even then. [xlvii] Occasionally the whole applecart is thrown over, such as will happen on March 16, 2013 when the America Invents Act changes everything from a first-to-invent system to a first-to-file system.

It is difficult to overstate how important this change will be. It essentially means that the patent granting process has become so unwieldy and impossible to apply, with all the millions of pages of prior art history to determine what is patentable and what is not, what is innovation and what is not, what is obvious and what is not, in short: what is prior art and what is not – that even its staunchest supporters realized the whole thing had to be pitched before arbitrariness became too ridiculous for words. So many examples abound in the daily business news that even Congress has been demanding changes, although this area is one of many members' pet prerogatives, and a great source of campaign contributions.

> The global battle (between Apple and Samsung) dates back to 2009 with lawsuits filed between Apple and Nokia Corp. and it has since ensnared the industry's big players in litigation all over the world, providing fodder for critics of the patent system, including members of Congress. One common complaint: the U.S. Patent and Trademark Office and similar agencies have issued too many patents over the years, especially on software designs, and patent holders are clogging the courts with frivolous lawsuits. [xlviii]

While changing to first-to-file will make it easier to decide some cases, it could easily lead to more confusion and arbitrariness rather than less. Claim-jumping and fear of claim-jumping will almost certainly become endemic, as the rush to file frivolous claims intensifies, since the first to file should have the edge even if someone else was arguably the first to invent. This will force everyone in business to maximize legal process without necessarily creating any business value for the effort. And it will certainly give even greater advantages than they have now to big and rich corporations who can spend whatever they want, over small companies or individuals that might otherwise aspire to invention but cannot afford the legal expense. Consequently, there is no reason to suspect that the prime reason to have patents in the first place – to incent innovation – will improve as a result of the change. More likely, the change will only exacerbate the clogging up of innovation with useless effort and expense that has increasingly characterized the existing system.

In the business of trading systems and stock exchanges, the primary and frequently the only business determinant of success is the critical mass of customers. While lawyers always recommend applying for the maximum amount of patents and copyrights possible, seldom is the holding of intellectual property even a minor determinant of success or a meaningful refuge from failure. [xlix] Different industries may have different experiences. But there do not seem to be any examples that have reached the popular press where the innovation value to society of the patent system has exceeded the disvalue of its cost.

In any case, patent applications are not for the faint of heart, or poor. While the upfront application fees are not large, the application is only the beginning of a long process that essentially never ends and almost always involves very large legal bills. Even if a patent is granted, often after years of back-and-forth with patent examiners, there are often ex parte challenges to answer at the USPTO and then challenges in court. Further, to have a valid patent that can block infringers or command royalties often requires proactively suing violators. This can cost hundreds of thousands or millions of dollars, all of which are spent in constant uncertainty as to what the proper interpretations of the law are or will be.

Amidst this uncertainty, a further insult to the natural law concept of property comes from the fact that the government that runs this system is largely incapable of enforcing the patents and copyrights it confers. This problem begins by placing the burden of enforcement largely on the willingness of the patent or copyright holder to proactively sue infringers, a burden that is the equivalent of telling travelers to bring their own bodyguards to bad neighborhoods. The problem continues with the increasing difficulty of defining what a violation is due to the escalating complexity of the field. And it spins out of control when large segments of the relevant populations of potential infringers do not agree with or accept the determinations of the United States. For example, virtually the entire youth of America and most people in technology businesses in Asia do not agree that what the USPTO calls "intellectual property" is property in the traditional sense, meaning they should not copy or steal it.

While Apple's home court in San Jose, California was about to award it a victory over Samsung, Samsung's home court in Seoul was giving it a better result, [l] and shortly thereafter another court in Tokyo also sided with Samsung. [li] Each country has its own, slightly different IP laws and, given the general arbitrariness of the field, has lots of leeway to help the home team. That is at least partly why experts predict the Apple/Samsung court battle will last for many years as it plays out in many countries, by which time it will almost certainly be irrelevant whether valid patent claims can be based on such innovation trivia as rectangles with rounded corners (the San Jose jury said yes for the I-Phone, no for the I-Pad). [lii]

All of this means that patents and other intellectual property are at best arbitrary in terms of the protection they provide. They do not meet the minimum definition of simple and understandable that would qualify as protection of property under natural law. And even when officially valid in a legal sense, the capacity of the government to enforce these sole seller licenses or to redress grievances is rapidly disappearing.

But it gets worse.

The rationale for patents rests on three assumptions, all of which are false. First, it is assumed that inventors would not be inclined to invent without the lure of a government-protected monopoly as an incentive. Second, monopolies are assumed to be somewhere between problematic and evil, unless blessed by government through patents. Third, it is assumed that the administration of the patent system itself will not become so mired in red tape or other dysfunctions that innovation is harmed more than it is helped by the policy.

All of these assumptions are false. The patent system is not spurring innovation, it is dragging us backwards, as experience in the field of stock exchanges and trading systems mentioned above demonstrates, and as all the critics of the current system for issuing too many patents imply. Second, naturally occurring monopolies are not problematic or evil; they are good. It is the government-blessed ones that create problems. Third, red tape is not just an accidental result of bureaucratic process. It has become the non-accidental means by which the patent and antitrust elites maintain their power. Red tape is for all practical purposes, a deliberate policy.

Among the most telling signs of our pending demise as the go-to country for innovation are the takeover stories touting targeted companies' "patent portfolios." So easy is it to tie up competitors in interminable court battles over intellectual property, or to implicitly threaten to do so by the size of your patent portfolio, and so critical is it to protect your own company against such risks, that companies are now scrambling to acquire thousands of patents or patents pending that can be used as both offensive and defensive litigation armies against their competitors. [liii] The price of patents in these troves has risen fast and is now over $1 million per patent, although all but 5% of them, according to estimates, are not enforceable. Their primary value appears to be in preventing competitors from getting hold of them and mugging you in court. The larger your trove, the less vulnerable you will be to being mugged. "'This has been a gradual evolution of patents from simple legal assets to strategic financial assets,' said Mark Radcliffe, a partner at law firm DLA Piper who specializes in intellectual property." [liv]

This development is exacerbating the already serious harm to innovation that "patent trolls" are causing. Patent trolls are firms made up largely of lawyers and speculators that do no inventing or operating of patented technologies, but instead specialize in legalized extortion. They buy up collections of unused patents and patents pending in the hope that in the millions of pages of patents, patent pending applications and prior art history they will find a few words that can be used to intimidate new or existing companies into paying royalties on one of the troll's unused patents. The situation forces entrepreneurs into the patent maw, which drains resources while producing few if any inventions that become operational. But it can easily kill businesses that might have become operational without patents, and thus might have been able to satisfy customers and hire people. In other words, trolls can kill businesses of real value. But they have only litigation value themselves.

The emergence of litigation armies and patent trolls has finally exposed the fatal flaw in the patent system, which had been there all along and should have been obvious from the beginning. As a clear carryover from the system of royal privilege in which the kings of England doled out licensed monopolies to their cronies, the USPTO was established as a government monopoly on the granting of private monopolies, a highly suspect operation on its face, at least for a new society supposedly based on natural law. Any hope that patents granted by our representative government's bureaucracy would be less arbitrary than those granted by the king was heroic to say the least. And because the system has become through confusion, inconsistency and red tape entirely arbitrary, it is clearly incompatible with natural law now. We are locked in to a method for incenting innovation that is now strangling innovation. The trolls and their litigation armies with troves of patents epitomize the ruling elite that now directs the distribution of property in America. The only beneficiaries are the privileged insiders with the rarified expertise and crony connections to manipulate the system in their favor.

Even the tweaks and twists have multi-billion dollar effects, dragging in all the influence peddlers known as lobbyists to the U.S. Congress. How long should drug patents last before covered drugs become generic? How long should copyrights last before works go into the public domain? What to do with business process patents? Such issues increasingly engage not only the entire intellectual property community, but the full panoply of the nation's diplomatic and foreign policy resources, as well as its defense resources, as we ceaselessly, but with less and less success, seek to yoke the rest of the world to our regime.

Rather than continuing to beat our heads against the wall of international organizations that dismiss our claims and reject our methods, there is a much simpler solution, one that is consistent with natural law, one that naturally creates property that does not require a cast of thousands of bureaucrats and experts to define and defend, one that would allow our economy to soar again. Unfortunately, this solution is locked behind the other half of the patent problem: antitrust. But strictly in terms of the efficiency of a system for incenting innovation, it is worth fantasizing for a moment on what could be achieved if monopolization were legal.

The time and money spent on patent processing is at least 95% wasted, judging by the only 5% of patents in those troves that are said to be enforceable. In addition, since many patents that are applied for never issue, and many that do issue are never used or achieve any commercial success, the time and money spent on patents is actually much more than 95% wasted. In contrast, the pursuit of monopolies results in property that is defined by consumer demand as discovered by entrepreneurial effort. Since consumers' and entrepreneurs' efforts are voluntarily given in hope of a return, they require no wasted effort, no money spent on lawyers, no time writing patent applications.

Although the borders of property created in monopolies are constantly shifting, they do so in response to natural forces like changing consumer demands, new ideas, and competition. Not only is no time wasted on legal minutia to define and defend those boundaries, but because of network effects like lock-in, all of the time spent pursuing monopolies is borne by and considered time well spent by monopolists, who create the value of their property for themselves and society out of thin air and their own genius. So valuable is that property that, in spite of all the efforts of trustbusters to kill them, the greatest values in the stock market and the most critical pieces of our industrial infrastructure all came from monopolies and monopolization, including stock exchanges. There is no need to spend one minute of any bureaucrat's time to define the border of a monopoly. In fact, so well does monopolization define and defend its own boundaries that antitrust spends all *its* time trying to tear monopolies and their natural borders down.

If both patent law and antitrust were to magically disappear, we would find ourselves in an environment where natural law defined and defended property rights without the need for a single bureaucrat. Invention would soar. Entrepreneurial activity would soar. Stock market capitalization would soar. GDP would soar. Employment would soar. Just about everything would soar, except government. And so the next important point on the path to our current dilemma was the passage of the Sherman Antitrust Act of 1890, which outlawed private monopolies:

> Section 1: Every contract, combination in the form of trust or otherwise, or conspiracy, in restraint of trade or commerce among the several States, or with foreign nations, is declared to be illegal.

> Section 2: Every person who shall monopolize, or attempt to monopolize, or combine or conspire with any other person or persons, to monopolize any part of the trade or commerce among the several States or with foreign nations, shall be deemed guilty of a felony.

The arrival of Sherman's formal restraints on private monopolies reaffirmed the USPTO intellectual property regime, including patents, trademarks and copyrights (in a separate office) as the only legal path to a monopoly. No other government entity was allowed to offer them, and you couldn't create one yourself via a trust or other private arrangement. In practice, though, monopolies and monopolization kept cropping up and often, even after they were busted, the monopolists ended up far richer than anyone got from patents. Moreover, in the meandering path of court cases and practical applications of the law, and the many other laws and interpretations that attempted to define whatever it was that Sherman's Congress really meant, it became less and less clear what the law prohibited and what it allowed.

As mentioned earlier, in Robert Bork's *The Antitrust Paradox: A Policy at War with Itself*, Bork offers so many examples of the conflicts and incorrect interpretations in antitrust that he often seems ready to scrap the whole enterprise. Others have reached similar conclusions. But while Bork and other critics of antitrust come from different perspectives, they have all fallen into the "denial defense" trap, and have thereby thrown monopolies and monopolization under the bus in order to get their clients off the hook. They defend against charges of monopolization by first acknowledging monopolization is something that can and should be controlled by antitrust, and then go on to say that their client is being falsely or incorrectly accused. [iv] If they are successful in their denial defense strategy, they will get their client off the hook, either because they will convince the court that their client didn't monopolize, or because they will convince the court it is misconstruing applicable antitrust law. But none of these antitrust critics can acknowledge the positive benefit that comes from network formation due to monopolization, because this would be tantamount to an admission of guilt by their clients, the accused monopolists.

As a result, no one defends monopolization, either as an economically beneficial act, or as a natural right of property. Instead, everyone defends antitrust. The left defends it for its promised redistribution effects, while the right defends it for its supposed efficiency effects (even as they disclaim any redistribution motives). And the critics of antitrust ironically provide the strongest support of all for antitrust, since every one of their denial defense arguments starts by acknowledging the basic validity of the antitrust concept. Not since bloodletting have experts been so sure of themselves, or unanimous in support of a bad policy.

There is a simple and naturally correct explanation for the confusion, conflicting interpretations and controversy. The reality is that antitrust has all along been attempting to do something that is profoundly foolish, namely to criminalize normal and productive business behavior. Viewed from the perspective of natural law, all of the acts that were made illegal under antitrust belong within our natural rights to pursue happiness and to accumulate and keep property. Whether they are controversial or not, per se violations or not, all of them would be considered normal, ethical and productive business practices, were they not prohibited by antitrust.

By the standards mentioned earlier, under which the essential feature of natural law is that it is not arbitrary, and is simple and easy to understand, antitrust fails on all counts. No one understands antitrust, and the experts are all over the map. This is obvious from the mere fact that companies regularly bet billions on deals that are as often as not rejected by authorities. Before the rejections, the protagonists and experts opine back and forth with bold claims of certain interpretations, what the law is, what the Congress meant, what the latest expectations are. And then the big surprise headlines come, rejecting the deal: Nasdaq barred from buying NYSE; Deutsche Börse barred from buying NYSE; AT&T barred from buying T-Mobile. Although some deals do go through, it is clear that nothing is clear going in. All deals could go either way at any point. This is the hallmark of an arbitrary law.

But the real question, where the rubber meets the road in terms of liberty and property rights, is this question: What does antitrust ask individuals to do or not do? Never mind the viewed-from-above effect of their actions, their combinations, their conspiracies in trust or otherwise. Just ask the question from the standpoint of the individual on the ground who is to answer it. Why is it, exactly, that I as a dealer in over-the-counter stocks can't agree with another dealer to charge the same commission and trade in the same increments? Why is it, exactly, that I can't agree with other members of a stock exchange to deal only on our exchange and to set a fixed commission and a fixed increment for trading? Why is it, exactly, that I and the members of my exchange can't agree to focus on new technology companies and also agree to not compete with another exchange that wants to focus on seasoned industrial companies? Why can't these different exchanges have different fixed commissions, different trading structures and different tick sizes? Fortunately for capitalism, there was no one around to tell the founding members of the world's main stock exchanges that they couldn't do such things. If antitrust had existed before stock exchanges, we would never have had stock exchanges in the first place, a scenario only Occupy Wall Street could love.

But similar questions could be asked more generally of practices outside the stock exchange sphere. Why is it, exactly, that the owner of a business or commodity is not able to lower or raise prices anytime he wants to for any reason? Why can't he agree with competitors to raise or lower prices together? Why can't a successful business in one sector use its success in that sector to help it enter another sector and be successful there? Why can't a business give better terms to good or large customers than to infrequent or small customers? Why can't a firm offer quantity discounts or, for that matter, discriminate in the prices charged for the sale of its product on any basis it so chooses? Why can't it offer better terms to customers who agree to not buy from its competitors?

Antitrust theorists, of course, have answers to all of these questions. But they are from the perspective of society as a collectivity, not from the perspective of the individual person in that society. For the individual to feel that he is doing something wrong if he engages in such acts, he would have to understand and agree on the mind-bendingly complex and tortured rationales that have been put forward over the years by elite theorists who claim the expertise to see things from above, but who in practice don't themselves agree on any of it. If the people in a society cannot understand and agree on the definitions of property and where the boundaries are, it is a stretch to imagine they could come together on how to abide by, much less enforce, property rights. In such a situation, the felt effect of the law cannot be anything but arbitrary and, therefore, the refuge in natural law from a community's inevitable conflicts is not feasible.

This problem cannot be solved by better education in intellectual property law, antitrust law or any other law. The very fact that the experts who have spent their academic, professional and commercial careers cannot agree, as the regular swings in the merger headlines prove, demonstrates the impossibility of educating the average citizen sufficiently to provide an agreed basis for property rights in these spheres. Moreover, if you dig deep into the issues, you will find the whole theoretical edifice is there only to keep the elite in business pretending to do something useful, something mysterious, something only they can understand. Like everything else government does these days, it all boils down to complex nonsense justifying redistribution, which is doubly nonsensical in this case, since antitrust purists like Bork claim that distribution should have nothing to do with antitrust anyway.

Time's Person of the Year in 2011 was The Demonstrator, a clear indication that property rights are in play everywhere, that natural law is nowhere to be found. One need not have an opinion, a Blue Team or Red Team view, to recognize that everything that matters is being decided at government levels that are out of reach to the people of the West; hence, the demonstrations. Supranational organizations of impossible acronyms wield great redistribution powers, the illegitimacy of which is only occasionally hinted by sensational headlines, such as those showing that the expert economist and former head of the IMF was regularly plied with prostitutes to get his attention. [lvi] The deficits of every nation, including that of the United States, are universally agreed to be unsustainable, a situation that was clearly caused by redistribution, but always invites and results in further redistribution. Is there a way out, a way forward that is not self-destructive? Is there way back to natural law?

To think this through, one has to begin with the fact that government is now the source of all definitions of property and that it is through this role that redistribution is unleashed and expanded. This role was developed in America in two stages. First, it was taken up indirectly through definitions and redefinitions of property, largely in such inscrutable bureaucratic processes as provided under intellectual property and antitrust regimes. Then, once it was clear that property was in play through such redefinitions, explicit redistribution was effected directly by taxes, entitlements and other flows that are subject to changes in political majorities. Theodore Roosevelt's New Nationalism is an example of the first stage, and Franklin Roosevelt's New Deal is an example of the second stage. The way was paved for the second, more brazen stage by the earlier unwinding of natural law that occurred largely behind the scenes through the meandering interpretations of intellectual property and antitrust laws of the first stage.

The primary party in interest here is not either of the warring factions alone, but government itself, which is enhanced by the debates between the Red and Blue factions. Whether redistribution swings upward or downward is of little consequence, as long as the governing elite stays in control of the process. Government's power swells with the anger and rage of the factions, and its control grows with the impenetrability of the debate. The more it turns on issues that are esoteric, nuanced and incomprehensible, the more government's role becomes unassailable. The more incomprehensible the issues are, the more they lend themselves to the emotional taking of sides, to beliefs that ridiculous solutions are, in fact, the answers to our problems. Incomprehensibility is the stuff of witch-hunts and crusades, wars and genocides, rabble-rousers and demagogues.

Few ideals are better suited to regulatory rabble rousing than that big is bad. Antitrust theory traditionally took no issue with size, per se, but instead held that monopolists were only guilty if they became large by engaging in one or more of the activities that were specifically prohibited, a determination over which authorities could often exercise discretion. But now in field after field, size is the new per se evil. In telecommunications, "net neutrality" theories aver that telecom is such an important sector of our infrastructure, and size such an un-remediable danger to it, that traditional antitrust discretion should be removed so that size can be blocked, period. [lvii] In the stock market, the SEC's National Market System is aimed primarily at knocking down big monopoly exchanges and big block dealers, which amounts to an effective per se prohibition on size. Ditto the Commission's new regulations targeting "large traders" as well as a slew of new market access rules, audit trail rules, and participant identification rules aimed at the same big traders. In the wake of the 2008 financial crisis, banks are targeted for size under the popular new phrase, "if a bank is too big to fail, it is too big." Under new and old theories, from fears of systemic risk to worries about the tragedy of the commons and lock-in, regulators are targeting size everywhere as the resident evil in modern society.

It doesn't matter what the theoretical justifications for these arguments against size are. The important thing is that they all involve complexities that can only be viewed by experts from on high, complexities that no average citizen could be expected to sort through, even if there were light at the end of these analytical tunnels. The murky arguments against size provide a perfect backdrop, separately and especially in the infinite confusion of their combinations, to the primarily Blue Team claim that government is here to protect us against size, just as it is here to protect us against unfair concentrations of wealth. The same backdrop is also perfect for the primarily Red Team claim that experts can be trusted to sort these things out, that they have the requisite theoretical and legal licenses to view the world from above, to know what to do. Thus all the nonsensical legal arcana wielded by the experts boils down to a campaign against success and size, per se, a position that fits in fine with the moral temper of the times embodied by Occupy Wall Street: Size is evil; Monopolies are evil; Inequality is evil; Something must be done!

Witch-hunts were not considered witch-hunts when they occurred. The crimes were assumed to be real, as were the witches. Prosecutions involved complex theories of human weakness allegedly resulting in real harm to the people, from infertility and impotence, to drought and Black Death. Experts debated how the witches caused such things, and often changed their theories. At one time it was heretical to believe witches flew on broomsticks. Later it was heretical to *not* believe it. Theories of guilt, trial strategy, interrogation strategy and interrogations were meticulously recorded, including the times, methods and costs of torture, which were billed to the witches' families, as was the cost of the wood for the fires they were burned in. [lviii] Whatever patent falsehoods they were accused of, their screams were real and gave real comfort to the people, who saw a church they thought was corrupt, finally doing something about the problems that plagued them. But in the end this important episode in history is best known for the term, "witch-hunt," because "five hundred thousand people had to die for crimes they committed in someone else's dreams." [lix]

6. Red, White, Blue

Modern witch-hunts don't seem on the surface to have the carrying power of the original, the capacity centuries hence to embody in a word what we are doing wrong now. But then the original didn't either, not until we started using "witch-hunt" metaphorically, which took centuries. [lx] Hopefully our current errors will become clear more quickly; we may not have centuries to figure it out this time.

Thousands of bust-the-rich headlines, from those featuring John D. Rockefeller, J. P. Morgan and Bill Gates, to the bankers, dealers and exchanges of today, convey hope that punishing the rich will cure the commoners' ills. The pillory seldom results in actual death, although the stress of public accusations in the Pujo Hearings may have hastened it for J. P. Morgan, [lxi] and the shame of it preoccupied John D. Rockefeller throughout the rest of his life, particularly in his relationship with his son. Rockefeller, perhaps the most moral and ethical of all American businessmen, and certainly the most successful in terms of the commercial value of the networks he launched and his own wealth, was also the most persistently and successfully vilified. [lxii]

The imaginary nature of the crimes the monopolists have been accused of, as well as the investigative methods of their inquisitors, are virtually identical to the made up charges and interrogation methods of the old Inquisition, sans the physical torture. Having a monopoly isn't supposed to be illegal in itself. If you got your monopoly only through hard work, for example, or if you merely lucked into a lock-in situation you didn't expect, you would be in the clear. But deliberately trying to get a monopoly *is* illegal, as is trying to extend one, or to keep one. For large businesses, almost any association with another person can be construed as deliberate monopolization by a sufficiently creative investigator. As could any admission or apparent awareness that your "hard work" or "luck" were directed toward monopoly opportunities. In practice, it would be unnatural, even inhuman, for a very successful person to not be aware of these things and how tilting activity toward them would help the business. It is easy to see why the charge of "greed" is so popular, as it implies an awareness of monopoly potential and thereby turns ordinary activities into illegal monopolization.

Such investigative methods always work at least to stop the monopolists in their tracks, preventing further growth and development of their enterprises, if not dispersing them or eliminating them altogether. Many of the greatest enterprises, from Rockefeller's Standard Oil to Bill Gates' Wintel, were blocked in the middle of their founders' careers, when they were relatively young men in their thirties or forties. So we will never know how great those enterprises could have become if they had been allowed to continue. And why were they blocked? Although the people can repeat the words – "conspiracy," "greed," "monopolist" – they are unclear as to how the inquisition's actions to root out these evils will benefit them, or how the humiliating fall of a successful man will improve prospects for the common man. Yet they cheer the bust-the-rich headlines, and some would no doubt relish seeing a few of those fat cats burned at the stake.

The imagined pain of others is not quite the same as witnessing it, cheering it, or causing it. The modern inquisition is only a distant cousin of the original, and a pale imitation at that. But a slight step back for a broader view reveals that man's inhumanity to man is alive and well in our time, too, and may yet eclipse the past. The redistribution wars of today, the Red Team/Blue Team debates, are only the latest manifestation of a conflict that has disrupted order and incited violence at least since Karl Marx pushed formal redistribution theories in the nineteenth century.

In the grand sweep, the establishment of a beachhead for liberty in 1776 soon ignited over a century of great growth in world wealth, reaching a crescendo with the network forming monopolies of the Robber Barons in the late nineteenth and early twentieth centuries, which, as Malcolm Gladwell described in *Outliers* and I noted in *War on Wealth*, were the richest people in world history. [lxiii] But great wealth also created a tempting target for redistribution. The socialist movements of the nineteenth century seemed to form in response to the beginning of this wave of wealth accumulation and hardened their insistence on redistribution as fortunes grew.

> In the early 19th-century, "socialism" referred to any concern for the social problems of capitalism regardless of the solution. However, by the late 19th-century, "socialism" had come to signify opposition to capitalism and advocacy for an alternative system based on some form of social ownership. [lxiv]

As the twentieth century dawned, socialism and redistribution were in the air and revolutions for change in property rights regimes began all over the world. The most important of these, given the source of the wealth and the political commitment to property that created it, was in the United States. Here, the Sherman Act and President Theodore Roosevelt's support for it under his progressive New Nationalism got the ball rolling.

There were ebbs and flows of wealth across the century, but the Robber Barons' feats were never equaled. The political march to redistribution and the unwinding of property rights persisted unabated, however, passing through President Franklin Roosevelt's New Deal programs and ending the century on President Bill Clinton's continued calls for "change," the best known and most frequently used code word for redistribution. The revolution in the United States was for the most part non-violent. The same cannot be said for those in Europe or Russia, where real revolutions, with guns, devastated those nations, conflicts into which the United States was also drawn.

History often portrays the twentieth century conflicts as disputes between nations, or as marches of madmen, or as inexplicable displays of racial intolerance. But these explanations never quite satisfy when contemplating the unprecedented scope of the devastation, or its persistence. Moreover, they tend to leave off with a sense of wishful relief, as if to say, *Phew – it's a good thing that one's over! Let's hope we never see another Hitler or Stalin again!* It is more complete to explain the twentieth century as a series of connected, continuing and perhaps escalating redistribution conflicts, both within and across nations, an explanation that better deals with their scope and more realistically leaves open the possibility for more, and worse, to come.

> Mass unemployment and the impoverishment of once-viable sectors led to populations in desperate need of food, clothing, and shelter. Desperate need inexorably led to war. Between 1939 and 1945, it is estimated, between fifty and sixty-six million people perished. Only someone unacquainted with, or oblivious to, the dark turns that history can take would say that such events are unrepeatable. lxv

It is also more realistic to view the men who led the devastation visited by armies, bombs and holocausts as creations of the historical situation, rather than as great men who drove it. There were organizational and structural similarities in how nations absorbed socialism and redistribution, even though they spanned across different, sometimes warring countries and emerged during different decades. The nationalistic embrace of industrial monopolies, both under Theodore Roosevelt's New Nationalism in America as well as under Adolf Hitler's National Socialism and Benito Mussolini's Fascism in Europe represented government grasps for control of the means of production and the power to redistribute that comes with it. The Third Reich's National Socialism had roots in the nineteenth century when the Second Reich's leader, Otto von Bismarck, a contemporary of Karl Marx, was known both for opposing socialism throughout his career and then for being the father of modern socialism via the social insurance programs he instituted, versions of which were also implemented by President Franklin Roosevelt in the United States that to this day form the core of official redistribution in America.

Bismarck's about-face illustrates the underlying reality: rather than being progenitors of new ideas that led their people to them, the careers of these men bear more resemblance to the formation of networks under power laws, as the most successful of them exploit the tempers of the times better than the rest, rising to dominance on the cheers of mobs for redistribution. The process is similar to how videos on YouTube go viral, as hits beget hits, or to how stock exchanges grow to dominance as liquidity begets liquidity. But these benign analogies belie the risks to societies and order when, un-moored from property rights, politicians go viral on promises of redistribution.

Redistribution doesn't just mean money. Rationales for redistribution can also gain force as ethnic arguments or using other crude and primitive markers of the enemy. Once the fear and greed of redistribution are in the air, each group increasingly self-identifies primarily by how it does not look or act or think or dress or pray like the other group. The mobs' basest instincts then feed on themselves in positive feedback loops, each reacting ever more strongly to increased threats from the other, leading in the end to situations where "fairness" demands disenfranchising and then segregating other religious, social, cultural, racial and other types of groups from society. At the extreme, such calculations of fairness will demand war and genocide, and there will be no end to the viciousness of the violence the groups will enthusiastically endorse against the "other."

There have been a number of genocides since the Holocaust killed six million Jews, all of which have happened since "never again" became the slogan of remembrance for that episode. In an effort to better understand why such horrors are still with us, network scientists and other authors have explored explanations for how ordinary people, including former friends and neighbors, can engage in inhuman brutality toward each other.

In *The Social Atom: Why the Rich Get Richer, Cheaters Get Caught, and Your Neighbor Usually Looks Like You*, Mark Buchanan recounts experiments that demonstrate the natural formation of hatreds to explain modern genocides, including an experiment by Axelrod and Hammond that uses only computer-generated behavior for people of arbitrarily assigned colors. Buchanan summarizes: "In a world of bigots, only bigots survive." [lxvi] What can create a world of bigots? Fear that those other bigots are going to eat your lunch. It doesn't take a genius to see that democracy itself, in the absence of property rights, could easily lead to a mob-rule condition that would incite such fear.

In *World On Fire: How Exporting Free Market Democracy Breeds Ethnic Hatred and Global Instability*, Amy Chua describes a series of modern genocides, among them:

> In the Serbian concentration camps of the early 1990s, the women prisoners were raped over and over, many times a day, often with broken bottles, often together with their daughters. The men, if they were lucky, were beaten to death as their Serbian guards sang national anthems; if they were not so fortunate, they were castrated or, at gunpoint, forced to castrate their fellow prisoners, sometimes with their own teeth. In all, thousands were tortured and executed. In Rwanda in 1994, ordinary Hutus killed eight hundred thousand Tutsis over a period of three months, typically hacking them to death with machetes. Young children would come home to find their mothers, fathers, sisters, and brothers on the living room floor, in piles of severed heads and limbs. [lxvii]

Chua and Buchanan give the lie not only to the hope that our genocide problems ended with Hitler, but to our assumption that winning World War II against the Nazis and the Cold War against communism somehow exempts us from being the cause of future such atrocities. Chua, in particular, fingers democracy and free trade as policies likely to ignite hatred of and revenge against "market-dominant minorities," which, as she demonstrates, "can be found in every corner of the world."

How is it that so many genocides have happened since "never again" became our official slogan? Hitler's emerged in a democracy where government took over virtually everything having to do with the distribution of resources and the organization of infrastructure in the society. Now we have a global competition of governments fighting over just such powers. Why would we expect a different outcome this time? And genocide may not be the worst thing such policies engender. In a world of proliferating technologies of mass destruction, there are bigger things to worry about than massacres with machetes.

One international agency, the World Health Organization, convened a group of 22 experts from countries around the world to determine whether to publish research into how to make H5N1 bird flu easily communicable among humans. It is not currently communicable among humans, but when humans get it from birds, it has a 50% death rate. The 1918 flu that killed 50 million people had a 2% death rate. The research, funded by the United States National Institutes of Health, reportedly demonstrates how to make H5N1 communicable among humans, like the 1918 flu was. The United States voted against releasing the report's findings on the recommendation of its National Science Advisory Board for Biosecurity. Some scientists, presumably from the United States or who were otherwise familiar with the study, were very concerned: "the research is so dangerous that it should never even have been done, much less published." [lxviii] The group of 22 experts at the World Health Organization, however, voted overwhelmingly to overrule the United States and release the study on the grounds that bringing more scientists in to study how to avoid the dangers of H5N1 as a weapon of mass destruction is needed. The study was published in Nature Magazine on May 2, 2012 ostensibly in order to allow scientists to develop vaccines before the terrorists develop their weapon of mass destruction. [lxix]

The Non-Proliferation Treaty (NPT) of the United Nations Office for Disarmament Affairs was opened for signatures in 1968 and has now been signed by 190 nations. Yet in spite of the NPT and the International Atomic Energy Agency (IAEA) authorized under it to monitor compliance, the risk of "losing a city," as Republican presidential aspirant Newt Gingrich phrases it, is clearly growing with the number of challengers that have slipped through NPT's and IAEA's cracks. These challengers are increasingly brazen in their defiance of the NPT and IAEA, and have been known to trade stolen secrets and whatever nuclear know-how they can muster with each other, motivated by their common interest in a world not dominated by what President George H. W. Bush called, the "New World Order," [lxx] nor that implied by President George W. Bush's "either you are with us, or you are with the terrorists" vision of the world. [lxxi]

As in the Axelrod and Hammond experiment with colors cited by Buchanan, the world is dividing into us against them, with those on the other side from the United States seeing red whenever they see the Red, White and Blue. In the global application of the Chua thesis, the United States itself is the market dominant minority, as all of its relatively rich people become just targets for the revenge of the world's oppressed and poor. Under these circumstances, it is suicidal of us to push us-against-them choices on the world, and yet that is exactly what we are doing. Us against them always catapults aggressive leaders' popularity upward, be it a Bush after Desert Storm or 9/11, an Osama bin Laden, or an Adolf Hitler. Us against them can only create more enemies of the United States, and more anger in each enemy.

If anyone thinks the United States is becoming safer for the us-against-them policy of the War on Terror, they should read the analysis of Seth Jones, who, although he is supportive of an aggressive stance, says nonetheless that the large troop deployments that have come to characterize United States policy are counterproductive.

When the United States and its allies have used overwhelming force and deployed large numbers of conventional soldiers, al Qa'ida has benefited through increased radicalization and additional recruits. [lxxii]

And if anyone still thinks the old MAD (mutual assured destruction) balance of nuclear power that protected us from a massive attack by the Soviet Union will work today against losing a city, they haven't been reading the final statements of the suicide bombers that are attacking us now or their religious justifications. A quick Google search of, "we love death as you love life" pops up 606,000 examples.

Still, the overall danger from Muslim terrorism is vastly exaggerated. Unlike the Soviet danger, or even Hitler, there is not now nor has there ever been any credible path by which Muslim terrorists, even with any budding nuclear nations helping them, could pose an existential threat to America. Yet the War on Terrorism posits just such an existential threat to the United States and its freedoms from Muslim terrorism. To many, that danger is real and immediate, and also carries with it a plan by Muslims to install Shariah law in the whole world, including the United States. This is nonsense. A few cranks on the fringe may encourage Muslims to dream about someday doing this in order to rally followers to jihad, but there is no credible path to such a plan's implementation. And in every case where the late Osama bin Laden or other acknowledged spokesmen for Islamic terrorists have opined on these matters, they have consistently said they are attacking us only because we are attacking them in their world. They want us to leave their countries, and will leave us alone if we do. There is every reason to believe them, since we would want the same thing if we were in their shoes.

But again, just because they can't take us over, doesn't mean they can't take out a city. That is the real danger, and it is one that is increasing with every day we continue the War on Terrorism, and it is increasing precisely because of the War on Terrorism.

For a nation founded on liberty, and particularly on religious liberty, it is ironic that we cannot recognize who is on the side of freedom now. With our perpetual wars in Muslim countries, with our propensity to force an us-or-them choice on every local population, with our leaders and spokesmen perpetually pushing views that conflict fundamentally with theirs, they are right: we are clearly the oppressors. This is not an un-American view. It is the view our Founders would have had. It is in fact the view our Founders did have when oppressed by English kings until we said we'd had enough in 1776.

As obvious as it is that we should drop the War on Terror before it kills more Americans, it is very unlikely that we will do so. Once these positive feedback loops get up a head of steam, it is very hard to reverse them. Like the domestic redistribution areas mentioned above, the War on Terror is also a field where confusion reigns, where experts implement policies based on theories no one understands. The occasional general on the ground who sees the light and speaks his mind is fired. The rare politician who broaches the topic is booed. The reality is that the only real danger we face from Muslim terrorists – losing a city – is a danger we are creating with the War on Terror. As to the other alleged dangers, they are fantasies concocted by neoconservatives and others whose careers depend on war.

The assumption that we will be made safer by thrusting our version of democracy on other peoples, that this will win their hearts and minds, is clearly false. This assumption is inconsistent with our own first principle of religious freedom, because it requires other people to accept our pluralistic, radical-egalitarian model, with all of its unsettled issues spinning out of control before our own Supreme Court, including our growing antipathy toward traditional religious morality and family structures. That we would presume to dictate how another society should treat women, for example, when our model has allowed the illegitimacy rate to rise from under 5% in the 1950s to over 40% now, with the critical category of women under 30 rising to over 50%, boggles the mind. [lxxiii] It doesn't matter if no one knows for sure what is causing this troubling trend. The mere fact that the illegitimacy rate is still soaring is reason enough for humility on our part and caution on theirs.

And remember, we are not just pushing this view to improve the lot of women in the world out of a belief that it is the morally or culturally right thing to do. This is a stated rationale for why the United States government is conducting wars, battling insurgencies, sending drones, killing people. We claim that pushing these egalitarian ideals *on other people* through violent wars is making us safer. Tell that to the families who lost 3,000 loved ones on 9/11, or to those who will lose many more loved ones if America loses a city. How many of them would agree that promoting feminism abroad under the guise of democracy is an American ideal worth losing that many lives for?

The connection between genocide and democracy is not accidental, as Hitler proved, and as Amy Chua and Mark Buchanan have demonstrated in recent contexts. These modern authors did not set out to paint this highly controversial picture, but paint it they did. In the absence of property rights, where the votes of mobs determine distribution, it may be that the most rational and logical strategy to secure the survival of your own group economically, as well as physically, is to try to exterminate the other group. The danger is highest where resources are most scarce, where group identities are most obvious through racial, religious or other easily recognized markers, and where property rights do not now and never have existed in the modern sense and were traditionally handled by tribal custom. In other words, the danger of genocidal atrocities due to democracy is highest in precisely those societies where the United States has been pushing its mob-rule version of it.

The elite leaders who push this policy would not agree that they are pushing a mob-rule version of democracy. They would insist that they are giving these budding democracies all available assistance in setting up constitutional protections for property and the legal institutions to support them. But since we have abandoned our own Constitution in this respect, how can we possibly expect that these more primitive societies will be able to embrace constitutional protections and keep them? Our own version has, after all, devolved into a group rights melee, with affirmative action or other preferences promoting ever more socially, morally and religiously controversial policies to help this or that group. Since our own people, and our own Supreme Court, are constantly at odds on such issues as to whether the alleged under-representation or suppression of women, minorities, homosexuals and others should be redressed through affirmative action or similar laws that give these groups special advantages, how could the societies we are trying to reshape through the War on Terror not get the impression that their societies will be torn apart too when we push these policies on them?

These policies are not truly rights-based. In the degree to which they force the increased insertion of one group into a society by elevating its advantages, they perforce undermine the representation, rights and property of other groups that have to make way for it. Even if we were settled on the wisdom of such policies in our own country, which we clearly are not, how can it be anything other than tyrannical to foist these policies on others? And again, we are not doing this only out of moral conviction, but pursuant to a strategy that is supposed to make us safer. But put yourself in the position of a devout Sunni Muslim in a majority Shiite country, like Iraq, or a devout Shiite Muslim in a majority Sunni country, like Syria. If you saw the U.S. democracy juggernaut coming your way, wouldn't you worry? Wouldn't you consider funding or otherwise supporting insurgencies? Wouldn't you want to reduce the majority's numbers before they democratically took away your rights and property? If you saw the enemy majority being sponsored, aided and abetted by the United States claiming to represent "universal law," "the international community" and "the world," wouldn't you wish for another 9/11?

It is not only arrogant of us to push democracy under these circumstances, it is deadly, perpetually causing tribal conflicts to erupt and spread. In effect, genocide and its little sister, ethnic cleansing, have become accidental policies of the West as we implicitly instigate their pre-emptive initiation in preparation for pluralistic democracy. Our policy, usually aided by the United Nations, NATO and various Western coalitions of the willing is to continue proselytizing and overseeing these conflicts and wars until the newly democratic societies are able to not only manage ballot boxes, but to grow the internal force to police their own pluralism. On current evidence it is much more likely that pluralism itself will be rejected before they succeed. Worse, the rejection process will tend toward civil war and unleash floods of refugees, destabilizing regions with calls for neighboring countries and the religious or ethnic divisions within them to take sides. lxxiv

We continue to be surprised and dismayed that these civil conflicts, like our own Civil War, are anything but civil. We should not be. We should not have such trouble imagining how much worse it would be if redistribution disputes weren't just about money or property, as they are in our wealthy country, but had large life and death consequences. If you thought your group would suffer large losses of its people if your ancient enemy took over the nation's resources under democracy, why wouldn't you engage in ethnic cleansing and genocide before democracy arrives? And how much more fervently would you fight if your group were the market dominant minority that controlled the country's resources? This would mean your group might go quickly from being the wealthiest to being the poorest, and could also have to suffer revenge attacks by the long-suppressed majority when it comes to power. And think too about the stakes on the other side, the majority's side, which, as Amy Chua describes, is already motivated to take revenge against the market dominant minority. Why wouldn't the majority want democracy just as much as the minority doesn't, and be willing to engage in equally desperate measures to get it? We really should not be surprised at the atrocities. When "freedom" is just a battle cry camouflaging life and death struggles over resources, when all it really means is to be free from dominance by the other side, we really should not be surprised at the atrocities.

All of the modern genocides have occurred since the United Nations was created to promote peace through democracy. But this was never logical. In the absence of property rights, democracy is bound to give way to mob rule, which is not only not likely to promote peace, it is a formula for civil war and genocide. The most favorable possible outcome of all of these West-inspired conflicts is that we will somehow find the trillions of dollars and willingness to take open-ended casualties that will be needed as we police this never-ending process of inserting democracy into countries that are at best not ready for it.

None of this is to say that these societies cannot develop their own workable versions of democracy, including their own workable versions of property rights. The Arab Spring is a hopeful development in this regard. But it will be subverted if the United States insists on meddling in every outcome, on regime changes, on blessing the right insurgencies, on running things. If we continue on this path, we will continue to be viewed as the oppressor, regardless of our intentions. We will not win hearts and minds; we will win enemies. Just because pluralistic, egalitarian democracies would not be likely to attack us, does not mean that forcing other societies prematurely, *in their view*, to adopt our model will make us safer. In fact, it is hard to imagine a policy that is more likely to cause us to lose a city.

Since our hopeful founding, Americans have with good reason seen their destiny as leaders of a march to greater freedom in the world and the global prosperity that would come as a result of it. Naturally, we believed that our destiny was in our control, and for quite a while, so it seemed to be. But in spite of our still dominant economic and military might, it is no longer clear that we are masters of our destiny. Rather, although we defeated two socialist empires in the twentieth century, it now appears that we are at least significantly swayed by the same errors that led them astray. No longer in charge, we appear instead to be bobbing helplessly at the front of the churning, breaking waves. If we do appear to be leading, it is only because we are the largest of the civilizations yet swept up in the redistribution tsunami, continuing into the twenty-first century the progression of the nineteenth and twentieth toward greater violence and chaos.

7. Red Tribe / Blue Tribe

Having adopted a mob rule version of democracy at home, Americans may witness up close how the Red Team versus Blue Team debates can turn violent when redistribution majorities threaten to swing. Tensions flare when elections highlight the stakes, and when signs of economic failure, such as the "fiscal cliff," force choices between political parties. These are the times when it feels certain that what you get in life depends on what the other side doesn't get, when anger matters most, at least as a political strategy, as making your anger visible is the way to get the attention of the politicians who appear to control the direction of redistribution. The inchoate violence of the Occupy movement has so far been outdone in other protests around the world, from the anti-globalization crowds to the European anti-austerity crowds to the Arab Spring crowds and the crackdowns they provoked. But we may catch up yet. One survey revealed that 31% of Occupy protesters would support violence to achieve their goals, [lxxv] and a number of Occupy offshoots, such as in Oakland, California, were soon making good on those implicit threats.

There are three forces to consider when contemplating the possibility that these debates will turn violent, all of which speak to the instability and unpredictability of the situation. First, the positions of the Red Team and the Blue Team are inherently irreconcilable. Over time, that irreconcilability is bound to foster increasing anger and a primitive instinct for revenge. Second, the international dimension of the debates, driven now by the War on Terror, is as open-ended and uncertain as any war. Through its visible examples abroad of violence and atrocities, it has the potential to insert copycat revenge-demanding incidents into domestic protests at any time. Third, while still the nominal advocate of liberty, in actuality the United States is lining up as the twenty-first century successor to the two principal tyrannies that led to millions of deaths in the twentieth century, namely Hitler's Germany and Stalin's Russia. As a consequence, instead of being a force for stability, America is becoming a cause of instability in the world.

The stakes in the redistribution wars are ratcheting up due to the collapsing economies of the West. Crises caused by politicians who promised more than their countries could afford are leading to unemployment and bankruptcies, as well as the possible breakup of the Euro and, as predicted by many in America, the drastic devaluation of the U.S. dollar through bailout-fed hyperinflation. These possibilities may be remote, but the very fact that they are being discussed endlessly and predicted by many experts is inserting urgency into distribution questions as citizens at all levels of wealth are forced to imagine the sudden disappearance of their savings. Today's predictions of hyperinflation hearken back to how the economically crippling reparations payments of the Versailles Treaty after World War I led to hyperinflation in Germany and Hitler's rise. History doesn't repeat, they say, but it rhymes. The next iteration of these trends probably won't see hyperinflation in Germany, death camps for Jews or, for that matter, hijacked airliners. But the possibility that something worse, potentially far worse, might yet emerge from today's spinning gyres is certainly growing.

A look at why socialism seems destined to lead to grasping, unyielding empires that cause millions of deaths before they collapse is in order. In the absence of natural law and property rights, there seems to be an irresistible tendency toward increasingly powerful socialist governments that justify control of all things on the presumed redistribution imperative. Such governments sprout demagogues that exploit fear and greed, inspiring primitive tribal behaviors that lead to unspeakable acts. However mild mannered and well intentioned the redistributionists seem at first blush, at full flower they are atrociously evil.

When Karl Marx died, his longtime coauthor and friend, Friedrich Engels said, "On the 14th of March [1883], at a quarter to three in the afternoon, the greatest living thinker ceased to think." lxxvi Socialism and Marxism are so often connected that modern observers might assume Marx originated the idea. No nineteenth century observer would make that mistake. However great his contribution to what socialism became and is still becoming, he did not start it. However great a thinker he was, he was not seminal. Marx's early life was driven by an intense desire to hook up with any of the many socialist movements that were already erupting all over Europe, just like Occupy today. The big question, then, is not how important Marx was to socialism, but why, well before Marx gained a following, socialist movements were springing up like mushrooms after a rain.

Marx had his theories, of course, prophesies of historical progression predicting the inevitable and imminent collapse of capitalism due to its excesses and inconsistencies, and its ultimate replacement by a classless society. According to his labor theory of value, the proletarian workingman had been getting shortchanged and would finally be getting his due. Others had theories, too, along similar lines.

Peter Kropotkin, writing in Russia, Switzerland, France, England and other countries a half-century after Marx and Engels wrote *The Communist Manifesto*, expected a modern version of something between a craft guild and a primitive commune to emerge where people took care of each other through "devotion and self sacrifice." lxxvii He thought this caring and sharing model could expand beyond its primitive and medieval roots, where everyone knew everyone else, to operate on a global basis under "anarchy," by which he meant without government control. Kropotkin provides many dramatic and persuasive examples of cooperation and order arising spontaneously in societies without direction from any government. While these observations could have taken him in the direction of natural law and property rights, Kropotkin went the other way. Unfortunately, his path leaves no logical link to how the habits of spontaneous order would re-arise if anarchists eliminated modern governments. At best, he implies that workers' solidarity or similar social bonds would somehow make up for the fact that a global community could not be based on personal relations and local decisions in the same way that communes and guilds were.

In the twentieth century many other versions of these theories were added, which alleged that society would function better with a variety of redistribution mechanisms in place. These ultimately included antitrust laws, minimum wage laws, equal pay for equal work laws, social insurance programs and many other schemes to spread the wealth around. The rationales behind all such schemes implicitly claim that fairness will win out over greed, because greed is inefficient and, anyway, it is tired. They usually claim or imply inevitability due to the superiority of socialism or the inferiority of capitalism or both. Though seldom as explicit as the phrase Marx used (but did not invent, as often thought), "from each according to his ability, to each according to his need," all of these programs seek that result or its equivalent in disguise. On the disguise front, "efficiency" came in particularly handy for those socialists who wanted to pretend they were capitalists, such as those in the antitrust cadre.

At their most radical egalitarian and doctrinaire, these programs assume people will work hard and well, regardless of what they are paid. Marx himself believed that much of the desire to work would come from the sheer joy of labor in a classless society. As to what people's needs were, he and his disciples thought it would be easy to figure that out, so easy in fact that government would eventually just fade away as socialism became classless communism. Besides, in this efficient flat future, there will be plenty for everybody, because those joyous laborers will be so productive that scarcity will never be a problem. Seriously, this is what they thought, and many still think.

The evident naïve absurdity of the socialists' claims, including those of "seminal" thinkers like Marx, invites comparison to other, far earlier claims. The many messiahs in biblical times, some of whom came before and some after Jesus of Nazareth, regularly gave rise to predictions of utopian empires that would last forever and look like the classless societies of Marx's communism. In such episodes, charismatic leaders take on the mantle of hope and prophesy to inspire followers to believe in and take action to bring about a leveling of society's inequalities, as described by anthropologist Marvin Harris in *Cows, Pigs, Wars and Witches: The Riddles of Culture*. [lxxviii] The eighth century BC prophet Isaiah, for example, inspired followers with words that will be familiar to fans of Handel's *Messiah*:

> Every valley shall be exalted, and every mountain and hill made low, the crooked straight, and the rough places plain. [lxxix]

Such beliefs, according to Harris, are rooted in primitive instincts of war that exhort followers to rally 'round leaders when a society is threatened or otherwise needs to defend or revolt against superior force. As an inducement to incite a fervent following, nothing works better than promising believers heaven on earth, often via metaphor. Our most popular modern metaphor, albeit less poetic than Isaiah's choice, is "level playing field," a term that never fails to rally socialists to hope and action. Harris's examples include the "phantom cargo" beliefs of New Guinea natives, who expect fleets of modern ships and aircraft organized by their ancestors to bring untold riches to the people and to vanquish their colonial oppressors:

> The dead and living will be reunited, the white man thrown out or subordinated, drudgery abolished; there will be no shortages of anything. The arrival of the cargo, in other words, will mark the beginning of heaven on earth. [lxxx]

Harris also describes how a millennium after Jesus, messiahs were still appearing, but with updated stories in which they were expected to defeat the Catholic Church and redistribute its wealth. Joachim of Fiore set several of these in motion.

> Sometime between 1190 and 1195, Joachim, who was a Calabrian abbot, discovered how to calculate when the present world of suffering would give way to the kingdom of the spirit. Joachim believed the first age of the world was the Age of the Father, the second the Age of the Son, the third the Age of the Holy Spirit. The third age was to be the Sabbath or resting time, when there would be no need for wealth or property, labor, food or shelter. [lxxxi]

Joachim's Third Age was to begin in 1260, ushered in by Holy Roman Emperor Frederick II. Unfortunately, Frederick died in 1250. But that did not stop the messianic predictions, which then began to include Frederick's return as well as in some versions Christ's return. Such predictions persisted for several hundred years, refreshing themselves with new dates when a date was missed, as 1260 was, and new versions of Frederick or persons similar, if needed. One of these, told in a sixteenth century document, the *Book of a Hundred Chapters*, predicted:

> Frederick was coming on a white horse to rule the world. The clergy from the Pope on down would be annihilated at the rate of 2,300 persons per day. The emperor would also massacre all moneylenders, price-fixing merchants, and unscrupulous lawyers. All wealth would be appropriated and turned over to the poor; private property would be abolished, and all things would be held in common: 'All property shall become one single property, then there will indeed be one shepherd and one sheepfold.' [lxxxii]

The reason the evident absurdity of such belief systems, when viewed from the outside or from the perspective of history, is not apparent to the society that is being rallied by it is that strong belief was effective in an evolutionary sense. The more absurd the belief, the more unified and aggressive its believers would be, provided they did not recognize or acknowledge its absurdity. The aggression that a strong uncompromising belief system evoked gave societies the capacity to win militarily over societies with less absurd and therefore less aggression-supportive belief systems. Strong self-identification and the resulting unified determination of a primitive people enhanced its fitness to survive in the degree to which its belief system was *not* rational. Irrationality blocked non-believers from mingling with or otherwise diluting the aggression of the believers. Irrationality also blocked apostasy among believers, requiring consistent in-crowd behaviors.

We can see the modern carryovers of such irrational habits of thought in all manner of customs, from the reflexive "Heil Hitler" salutes of Nazi Germany, [lxxxiii] to the politically correct attitudes that seek to eliminate the differences between the sexes in America today, to the violent suppression of such Western attitudes by the Taliban in Afghanistan that seeks to keep the sexes separate and distinct. [lxxxiv] Just as the best protection against being called a witch and burned at the stake was to accuse and call for the burning of other witches, these strange habits serve to separate friend from foe, to rally your group against the other group, and to protect you from attack by your own group – provided you buy into the story, or at least convincingly say you do. And they work not in spite of the fact that they are irrational, but because they are irrational.

Why socialism should prevail as a rational economic, political or social schema has proved difficult, indeed impossible, to explain, and all of its advocates, including Marx, have failed at it. But explaining why socialism has had repeated appeal as various charismatic leaders have led new forms of it over the centuries is not hard. It is basically a religious belief with roots in the primitive instincts of war, and its survival value lies precisely in its incoherence. As to why it has shown up with such strength and persistence in modern times, all of the tortured dialectic theorizing by Marx and others pales before the simple explanation that Willie Sutton gave as to why he robbed banks: because that is where the money is. The great success of the liberty-based economies in Europe and America created so much wealth that inequality grew to a degree and visibility that were unprecedented. This was the rain that caused the socialist mushrooms to spring up everywhere in the West.

While those socialist mushrooms were rooted in primitive instincts of war, the societies that have taken up socialism in the West today are not threatened in any way similar to how the societies in which those instincts first gained expression were threatened. Nor is there any equivalent need to revolt against colonial oppressors, the Catholic Church, the kings of England or France, the feudal system, the landed property system, serfdom, slavery or any of the other institutionalized protectors of accumulated wealth that gave birth to those spread-the-wealth messiahs. As anyone with an Internet connection or a television set knows, many paths to wealth for both individuals and nations are available now, and those opportunities are growing apace with no need for violent revolution to create them. Hard work and luck maybe, but not revolution.

In fact, the opposite is true: it is the socialist regimes in the West that stand in the way of prosperity and wealth for their citizens. While a revolution against *them* would make sense, it would be based on the opposite principles from those of socialists like Marx: natural law, rather than the overturning of natural law; rationality rather than irrationality; common law and the rule of law rather than mob rule; the rights to life, liberty and property, rather than redistribution by arbitrary government. But the socialists cannot go there, because the governments of the West are essentially what the socialists have always called for, or at least the closest practical approximation of it. The lunatics are running the asylum. Their cries for "change" are out of place, therefore, something between loose cannons and unguided missiles instinctively and irrationally seeking revenge against wealth in an institutional environment that, oddly, lauds their efforts.

But this makes them all the more dangerous. The primitive wars that shaped their instincts were ritualized and quite contained, following scripted protocols that prevented vengeance from getting out of hand and destroying those societies. [lxxxv] The global conflicts that are possible today would not be so contained. We have long since dropped the primitive protocols of war, and the modern ones that have replaced them are more likely to promote vengeance than to contain it. Another difference: weapons of mass destruction.

There is an obvious risk that the primitive instincts that seemed to help early societies survive may not transplant well to modern times. If we are headed toward an extension into the twenty-first century of the unspeakable, atrocity-laden conflicts of the twentieth or, worse, some kind of nuclear Armageddon, whose fault will it be, the Blue Team's or the Red Team's? That's a tough one. The truth is that socialism is a bipartisan project. While the Blue Team may focus on food stamps and the Red Team on bailouts, between them they represent virtually 100% of the population in favor of socialism.

When government sets itself up to manipulate outcomes, not only does everyone in the realm have a natural beef with its choices, but there is a lot of old-fashioned stumbling, bumbling and Keystone Cops confusion as to what the effect of it all is. Plans to remake wealth distribution, or the structure of markets or industries or the family, have a good chance of turning out differently than intended, and seldom better. When government makes changes, it is implicitly saying that we cannot trust the choices of a free people, because the world is too complex to leave important things like income distribution or stock exchange structure to chance or natural evolution. This is economic and social eugenics. It is bound to fail, because nature is capable of handling complexity far better than government. In fact, the overwhelming majority of complexity that exists comes from natural network formation, such as occurs during the evolution of social and economic structures. Government cannot possibly catch up. But it can screw up without breaking a sweat.

Imagine if our modern government had had a look at the treatment of women in some of the savage societies described by Harris, where male brutality toward women and female infanticide were common. We quite naturally would have wanted to apply a little feminism to the equation, a little equality versus the males. But those societies might have died out as a result of our premature women's rights revolution. Habits of brutality, including toward women, were necessary, according to Harris, for rearing the fierce warriors whose battlefield conquests enabled their tribes to survive. And female infanticide kept the total population that included all of the competing tribes within the bounds of their limited forest resources, primarily of food. [lxxxvi]

Brutal and primitive as such practices were, the same Darwinian evolution that led to them leads naturally in time to more civilized practices. Perhaps the best proof of this is that, except for a few isolated pockets, those primitive societies have all died out. Fascinating and instructive as they are, Harris's examples exist today (or did in 1974 when he wrote *Cows, Pigs, Wars and Witches*) only because they were shielded by their isolation from recent evolution, not because they participated in it. Such societies and their brutal practices have disappeared because more advanced and civilized practices competed with them, and the primitive practices lost the competition. As even anarchist and socialist Peter Kropotkin demonstrated, Darwinian competition is a *civilizing* force, relying on instincts of "mutual aid" and cooperation, rather than a "bitter struggle for the means of existence, among animals of the same species," as was assumed by others, "(though not always by Darwin himself)." [lxxxvii] Not only has our mutual-aid instinct evolved to allow man to rise above the other species, the same instinct and process have led within our species to ever more civilized and orderly structures. So much for "red in tooth and claw." Darwinian evolution tends to lead away from brutality or exploitation, not toward them, as critics of "social Darwinism" often contend.

Kropotkin believed in "anarchy" because he saw that mutual aid, cooperation and order developed spontaneously, without direction by any government. The process of evolution – free of government direction – allowed complex social structures to emerge based on ethical principles that restrained "passions." lxxxviii Although, as mentioned earlier, it is unclear how Kropotkin expected socialist societies to maintain that spontaneous order, or create a new order to replace it, he was closer to natural law than his Western critics might assume. Anarchy to Kropotkin meant the unhindered state of nature that allowed order to emerge spontaneously, a view that is consistent both with network science today and the political philosophy of the Founders of America.

The human bondage that followed primitive wars, and the abuse of women by primitive men, are examples of practices that tend to die out naturally as better means of securing resources for the strong compete with those crude old methods and drive them out of existence. In addition to providing better options for the strong, this process provides new ways for the weak to secure food and shelter for themselves without submitting to humiliation or exploitation or brutality. Darwinian competition among social and commercial structures will thus naturally eliminate institutions such as slavery and brutality toward women. New arrangements will progressively replace old ones that depended upon dominance of the weak by the strong, as the strong move on from owning slaves toward hiring employees, or from brutalizing women toward treating them chivalrously.

And the improvements don't stop with the elimination of the most brutal and primitive conditions. At every stage of human development, and at every level of society's wealth, there will always be some who are weaker than others, or poorer, or less capable, or less experienced, etc. These people may feel or actually be dependent on or subjugated by or even brutalized by the strong ones, the dominant ones, the masters, the bosses. But at every stage there is also the potential for new structures to emerge that will compete with and ultimately eliminate the older, cruder structures, providing in the process an ever-widening array of satisfying options for employment that do not make the employed feel dominated or subjugated.

The primary reason the new structures will emerge is that they make more efficient use of available labor resources, as people competing for opportunities to be employed, or to be employed for greater compensation, will work harder, more creatively and more effectively than those who are subjected to humiliation, slavery or brutality. Ambitious bosses will serve their own interests by making creative use of such competition. Expanding modes of human interaction will ultimately develop exchange, trade and commercial networks that offer vastly more varied employment options for the weak and formerly dominated people, as well as better opportunities for the strong to expand their enterprises. There is in fact no end to the potential for the human condition to be improved by such evolution, as long as government does not get in the way of the human interactions that give rise to it.

The slaves will get jobs, and the plantation owners will go on to build the expanding agricultural corporations and other types of companies that hire them. Eventually, the descendents of the owners and the slaves will compete virtually indistinguishably at all levels of the countless future enterprises that will be created by this process.

No government actions or designs or suggestions or incentives or coercions of any kind are needed to bring these felicitous developments about. In fact, government is the one thing that can prevent their natural unfolding. In spite of this, unfortunately, governments are wont to interfere with the freedom of people to interact naturally, as their improvement and progress require. Historically, governments grew out of the war activities of primitive peoples, and naturally fell into legal and administrative roles that perpetuated the slavery that followed wars, as the victors put conquered people to work as slaves or conscripts – and went on to new wars.

Over the centuries, governments have been creative as they added roles that only government, according to government, had the expertise or scale or position to administer. From defense to education to delivering the mail, from utilities to telephones to space exploration, from solar power and electric car batteries to basic research, from the tragedy of the commons to the EPA to global warming, from health care for the elderly and poor to health care for everyone, from patents and antitrust to running monopolies under "deregulation," from a "national energy policy" for converting corn to ethanol to a National Market System for trading stocks – the excuses for government prerogative are endless. This is all very different from what the Founders envisioned. While they may not have been quite yet ready to imagine doing without a post office or a patent office, they were clearly trying to free up the people to explore the possibilities on their own. They were looking for ways to do without government, not looking for new roles to lock government into. Unfortunately, as anyone can see looking around at what our government is involved in today, the restraint on government's activities our Founders hoped for in 1776 is nowhere to be seen.

This is most clearly the case in the field of war, the original and most enduring excuse for government prerogative. Now, instead of only protecting the people and the nation against external attack as a matter of self-defense, the United States is applying its military and diplomatic assets in attempts to remake the world in its own image via "nation building." Although these two roles – the self-defense role and the nation-building role – are often conflated, or implied to be one and the same, they are not. While the self-defense role almost certainly does make us safer, the nation-building role has the opposite effect. It has already cost thousands of lives and trillions of dollars. [lxxxix] And through its insistence that other peoples adopt the new American principles of democratic pluralism, which are contrary to their cultures, nation building is creating the terrorism it is meant to suppress.

The nation-building role is of a piece with our general situation today, in which government intrudes into every aspect of our lives. This is a condition our Founders would have recognized as tyranny. It will come as a surprise to most Americans, then, to learn that it was President Lincoln, "the great emancipator," who set us on this course. Few Americans are aware that it was the Civil War that led to all of these excuses for government that are now so contrary to the nation our Founders envisioned. The Civil War was our first "national conversation" that set the pattern by which government now intrudes into every aspect of our lives. Although today's national conversation is no longer only about race, it still largely is. And it still sets the pattern in which all contenders vie for a claim on national respect – white labor, black labor, labor, union labor, non-union labor, small business, women, elderly, veterans, immigrants, Hispanics, Asians, students, Pell Grant recipients, Head Start recipients, farmers, milk producers, homeowners, subprime victims, teachers, the middle class, the 99%, etc. Everyone has a claim and everyone is mad because they think others are getting more than their fair share. The angry tone of self-righteous entitlement is all that remains of the moral clarity of emancipation, as the original national conversation about race expands to include an infinite number of other national conversations, all seething with conflicting claims, too, and all getting further and further away from resolution as the nation gets further and further away from its founding principles.

Slavery could have been resolved in a manner that was consistent with freedom, such as by removing support in our national laws for the institution of slavery. By declaring, for example, that the unalienable rights of all men to life, liberty and the pursuit of happiness were superior to any claims alleging ownership by some humans of other humans, our government could have done what was in its power to remove impediments to freedom, and could have done so without going to war. But President Lincoln took us on a different course that pushed America back toward tyranny.

Although the Civil War removed slavery, doing so via war put government back in control of our destiny, blocking the people's freedom to interact that would improve their condition naturally. While mandating the emancipation of slaves sounded like freedom, in reality creating freedom by mandate and war foreclosed the possibility of resolving slavery through the natural competition and evolution of social structures. Rather than simply removing laws that supported slavery, and letting the South secede if it wanted to, the United States forced the whole country, including the South, to adopt its rules in its first nation-building war. That choice set America on a path that abroad is less about liberty and more about global conquest. And at home it has blocked our fundamental rights at the critical junctures when the protection of those rights would have been most beneficial.

Among the losers from that choice are the former slaves and their descendents, whose progress was blocked all along the way – and is still being blocked – by the Civil War and its legacies. The war created the paradigm of the Red Team versus Blue Team debates by which the distribution of wealth and the life prospects of different groups are still being determined by government. Emancipation by mandate and war were the original and most forceful of the Blue Team's downward redistribution initiatives. The Red Team countered quickly, also forcefully, fighting back first via the Confederacy, then after the war via the Ku Klux Klan, Jim Crow laws, segregation and various other forms of formal and informal discrimination. To which the Blue Team came back with civil rights, desegregation, busing and a variety of programs designed to give special help on a racially discriminative basis with affirmative action. The backlashes and the counter-backlashes over affirmative action, and all the extra anger over entitlements and tax rates and other distribution issues that energize the Red and Blue teams today, are the legacy of having settled slavery via violence and coercion rather than liberty.

That legacy is spreading now from our nation to the world. Racial tensions and the general sense of self-righteous entitlement on both sides of every divisive issue are infecting disputes of other races, regions and divisions of the world as the United States forces its coercive model of government on others. Our Civil War has thus inspired what amounts to a global civil war, or a "war of civilizations," as it is sometimes called, as the Western rules for society and war are forced on the world through diplomatic pressure and the War on Terror.

The modern rules of war, such as the 1949 Geneva Conventions, are the righteous core around which America's moral claim to organize the world is fashioned. These rules of war are rooted in President Lincoln's Emancipation Proclamation of January 1, 1863, according to Yale Law School professor John Fabian Witt in an op-ed piece in the New York Times. This, too, will come as a surprise to most Americans, because it is a part of our history that, according to Professor Witt, "few Americans know anything about."

> Drafted by the Columbia professor Francis Lieber and approved by Lincoln himself, the code set out a host of humane rules: it prohibited torture, protected prisoners of war and outlawed assassinations. It distinguished between soldiers and civilians and it disclaimed cruelty, revenge attacks and senseless suffering. Most of all, the code defended the freeing of enemy slaves and the arming of black soldiers as a humanitarian imperative, not as an invitation to atrocity. The code announced that free armies were like *roving institutions of freedom*, abolishing slavery wherever they went. [xc] [Emphasis added.]

The code was hastily attached to the Proclamation before it went into effect to quell the uproar in the South and in Europe over the possibility that freeing slaves in a territory Lincoln did not yet control would invite atrocities of revenge against Southern slaveholders. Atrocities were not supposed to be part of civilized war. Whatever their tempering effect, the new rules provided "a way of advancing the Emancipation Proclamation and of arming the 200,000 black soldiers who would help to end slavery once and for all," as described by Witt in his book, *Lincoln's Code*. [xci] Although no general slave insurrection occurred, by deploying black soldiers against their former masters, the policy incited an expectation of atrocities [xcii] and inspired counter-atrocities by Confederate soldiers who viewed the code as authorizing uncivilized war. [xciii]

In addition to the code that underlies the protocols of modern war, the Proclamation left two other legacies. Witt mentions one of these, with all due ominous presentiment. It is that the encouragement of a slave rebellion in an enemy's country, with or without atrocities, became an accepted tool of war.

By authorizing freedom, the new code also licensed a powerful and dangerous war strategy. It was a tool of the Union war effort, like the Springfield rifle and the Minnie ball. [xciv]

The third legacy, unmentioned by Witt, is the precedent the Proclamation set for the official encouragement of any class of dissatisfied people in a rival's society to rise up and rebel against its ruling regime. While slavery is the particular case the Proclamation addressed, it wouldn't take many lawyers to figure out that that precedent could also be applied more generally wherever one society thinks another does not have its various groups and people living under the proper arrangements and relationships to each other. We hear the modern echo of that precedent in the constant calls in America for our government to officially support and encourage "our side" in every foreign conflict or rebellion, whether or not we can find any legitimate American self-defense interest in the situation. And while the nostrums in Lincoln's code might give political cover to any apparent intent of the policy to cause these encouraged uprisings to turn into vengeful atrocities, the reality is that they are all bound to. No rampaging ex-slaves or machete-wielding Hutus or Serbs slaughtering Muslims will give a moment's thought to feckless post-war trials when they are in the heat of their struggles, nor will they pay attention when our leaders brag about bringing perpetrators to justice or holding them accountable.

And so it came to pass that in spite of our rules supposedly governing civilized war, and in spite of the reputation of emancipation as "the greatest moral triumph of modern political history," [xcv] together they set the stage for America's demands that others adopt our version of democracy, demands that have themselves become the primary provocation to war and vengeful atrocities in our world today. And the atrocities go both ways. It is not just the "roving institutions of freedom," but also the reactions to them that can horrify us, such as when the Taliban shoots a schoolgirl who promotes Western values like education. [xcvi]

For our part, we celebrate the girl on our front pages and talk shows so neither side can misunderstand the divisions. While we can easily point to the Taliban and al Qaeda as the proximate perpetrators of such atrocities, the West bears some responsibility in these incidents. In *this* war, they are *our* versions of Lincoln's roving institutions of freedom. We bear responsibility because we have encouraged them to rebel against their societies and take our side. However right or righteous our view might be in the long run, we cannot escape the reality that they are being murdered now for taking our side. And for all our losses of blood and treasure, we have failed at shielding them from atrocities, because the civil order enforced by U.S.-trained police and armies that we promised has not materialized, and is unlikely to before we leave. [xcvii] Having fomented rebellion with dreams of equality, we will soon abandon those rebelling schoolgirls to the Taliban.

The modern protocols of war, including the Geneva Conventions and all of the other pious moralizing emanating from the Untied Nations and other multinational assemblies, have tacitly accepted Lincoln's proselytizing model of creating roving institutions of freedom around the world. But whether these institutions have created freedom or conflict among proselytized peoples, as protocols for civilized war, they have utterly failed. In fact, they have only made modern war both more likely and, if engaged, more likely to be barbaric. Instead of restraining vengeance, these pretentions actually authorize the encouragement of divisions within societies that are bound to result in vengeful atrocities, covered over only by the fig leaf of prospective post hoc war crimes trials.

The Emancipation Proclamation's two parts each put us on a self-destructive trajectory toward government intervention. The emancipation part, for all its high moral reputation, was in practice an invitation to atrocity, a deliberate attempt by a President, perhaps desperate to recover from initial losses in the war he started, to incite vengeful slave rebellions in enemy territory. The other part was the code of war that supposedly would restrain those atrocities, but in fact was a feckless fig leaf that never could, and was almost certainly never expected by President Lincoln to, actually restrain them.

Today the emancipation part has generalized from freeing slaves to promoting rebellions, but has retained its actual central purpose of inviting atrocities. The feckless fig leaf part is still useless for restraining atrocities, but has grown into a massive multi-national bureaucracy to maintain the pretense of restraint through processes run by the United Nations and war crimes tribunals. Thus the code now provides the moral authority under which "the world" demands adherence to its dictates and the United States forces us-against-them decisions on other countries. Not only is the feckless fig leaf of multi-national process causing the separation of civilizations as the rivals square off against each other in the War on Terror, it is forcing renunciation of traditional and effective means of self defense that actually work. By requiring disputes to be resolved only through international consensus, the right of self-defense that *can* restrain aggression and atrocities has gradually been emasculated and outlawed.

No primitive savage, according to Harris, needs anything more than the memory of past injury by an enemy to come up with an excuse for a new war, and the motive is always revenge. [xcviii] But Harris's savages were lucky: they observed scripted protocols in their wars, restraining the damage revenge could do to civilization. We will not be so lucky. Attempts to prematurely impose a developed society's rules on one that is less developed could have disastrous consequences. Not the least of these is that war between two civilizations at different stages of evolution could unleash violence far beyond what either of them can imagine, in which the advanced weapons of the developed society are brought into play unrestrained by any scripted protocols of war that either society on its own might have been able to rely on.

The tragic irony is that any such clash that occurs would occur because the developed society insists on imposing interventions on both societies that are preventing either of them from developing further through natural evolution. We are imposing our new ideals of pluralistic egalitarian democracy on societies that cannot now and may never be able to accept them without civil war. This shouldn't surprise us, because we couldn't either. We fought our own Civil War over the original formulation of those very ideals.

With minor exceptions over tactics and terminology, both the Red Team and the Blue Team are committed to waging the War on Terrorism, but in their own ways. The differences that separate them lie properly only in the realm of nuance, as the arguments hinge on minor issues like the tactical value of surges, or the wisdom of announcing withdrawal dates, or on whether to focus more on Afghanistan or Iraq, counter-insurgency or policing. But the political battles over these issues take on allegedly existential significance as each team says all hope for the American way of life will be lost if the other team's Warriors on Terrorism are chosen at the next election. In their zeal to win political territory, both teams are incapable of noticing that the real threat to America is their nonsensical debate, and that that threat is indeed, ultimately existential. In the economic realm, it is destroying the potential of the economy to employ people and produce wealth. In the international realm, it is creating enemies that want to blow us up.

The policies coming out of the Red versus Blue debates, which are causing both economic failure and war, are inconsistent with the principles America was founded on. Even so, the question posed earlier is still difficult to answer: Whose fault will it be, if America goes down for the count economically or loses a city? While almost everyone would have an answer, few would be distinguishable from ordinary Red or Blue arguments fingering the other team for our ills. So for now, let's ask a different question: Is there a way for Americans to renew their vows to America's founding principles? The world is a fast moving place, and it seems sure that some country or group of countries out there will again find the way to that magical formula and initiate the next growth miracle by protecting liberty. Is there any chance that that country could be the United States of America?

8. The Second Revolution

If I could wave a wand that would command everyone to adhere to the U. S. Constitution, I would do so. The Framers created the best model for a government based on liberty that ever was, before or since, and if we could get back to it, we should. But there is a flaw in the Constitution that would render my fantasy moot, even if I could find that wand. And that is that the Constitution has failed at its principal mission, the reason it was written down. Although the Framers endeavored mightily to craft a work for the ages, one that would anticipate and block the tendency of government to encroach on liberty, we must admit that it no longer does so. We don't have to know why. All we have to know is that, after a two-century test, the Constitution no longer serves its primary purpose. As all Republican Presidential candidates imply when they say we have to get back to it; as popular books attest in detail; [xcix] as constitutional experts like Bork warned things might come to: constitutionally limited government is no more. Tyranny is back.

Or, to use the modern term, socialism is here. And it's not your garden-variety early socialism where hope springs eternal, where the good intentions of the naïve and foolish inspire expectations that "change" will actually be for the better this time. It's the late stage where things are unraveling fast, where anger and disappointment have long since extinguished hope, where getting what you can – redistributed from the other side – is all there is.

In *Crisis and Leviathan*, Robert Higgs demonstrated how government grows in response to crises. Because it never recedes back to where it was prior to the crisis that occasioned the growth, there is a ratchet effect that is cumulative and ultimately debilitating. [c]

While Higgs's argument was persuasive and powerful, the problem we face today is far worse than what he described in 1987. The history Higgs describes is of government riding to the rescue to solve crises that arise by and large independently. But that is not what we're seeing today, at least not primarily. Today's crises are not exogenous; they do not arise independently. Today, government is the cause of all the main crises it is expanding in response to. Government grows and grows, apparently having learned that it can accelerate its growth by perpetually creating crises that it then gins up new government solutions for, which then create the next round of crises. Not only is the ratchet still fully operational, there is never any settling back post crisis at all.

We live in a society where the recommended solution to all problems is some sort of government remedy. That being the case, we need to be prepared for the possibility that the remedies we are applying are in fact the causes of the maladies they are the alleged cures for. And not just in isolated cases where we just happened to get it wrong once or twice. It may be that in our zeal to justify past choices, we are locked into a pattern of self-justification across the board in which every aspect of our lives is being made worse by a government that is constantly ratcheting up the doses of the failed and failing remedies it has been applying all along.

Could we really be so stupid? Bloodletting was for 2,000 years the recommended remedy for almost all illness. Here was a case where the remedy was not just worse than the disease. This was a case where the remedy often *was* the disease. [ci] Apparently, the temptation to do something, rather than to just let nature take its course, is indeed capable of getting us humans to do incredibly stupid things sometimes – in fact, over and over again. Just as there was always some kind of illness or injury to justify bloodletting, there will always be some kind of inequality to justify redistribution. The only real difference is that, far from being a disease or aberrational in any way, inequality is a sign, perhaps the most important sign, of a normally growing and healthy society. But we must not think that because we began as a committed free country that understood and could tolerate inequality, we will always be one, or that somehow our history in liberty will save us from succumbing to the tyranny of redistribution now. We do seem, after all, to be mired in endless efforts to alter this natural condition with very unnatural cures, succumbing over and over again to the temptation to do something.

When Gwen Ifill of PBS's Newshour interviewed Paul Taylor of the Pew Research Center about the fact that our country is becoming more segregated by income in terms of where we live, the discussion centered around what a big problem this is and how it is getting worse. [cii] Not a word was mentioned about the possibility that this is a healthy development, indicating that America is still growing wealthier, enabling successful people at all income levels to do what they always do, which is to move up to better neighborhoods whenever possible. The fact that they are doing so can only mean that they are acquiring the wealth to make it possible. This is not bad news; it is good news. In fact, it is very good news. It is especially encouraging that the distribution of wealth and the distribution of income segregation by neighborhood are still fanning out, enabling people at all levels to increasingly identify what improvements in their lives would look like if they could afford them, so they can aspire to them. But none of this was detectable in the PBS story. The subtext was that this was just another sign of growing inequality that government must devise solutions for.

How did we get here? The temptation to do something about inequality via redistribution was there all along, including at our nation's founding. How did we manage to resist that temptation at first? And how did we lose the ability to resist it?

The eleven years between our Framers' signing of the Declaration of Independence in 1776 and the adoption of our Constitution in 1787 [ciii] were a time of continued ferment over philosophies of government. While the Framers wrestled with compromises that included the Bill of Rights, a necessary addition to secure ratification apparently, the French Revolution was brewing. In the written rationales for both revolutions, the more the scribes scribbled, the further they got from their original clear purpose. In France, the first version of The Declaration of the Rights of Man and Citizen in 1789 had some of the clarity of our 1776 Declaration of Independence, but wavered as well, apparently conflicted over what rights came from nature and were therefore inherent and unalienable, and what rights came from government and were thus malleable and arbitrary. The second version in France of the Declaration of the Rights of Man and Citizen in 1793 veered sharply in the direction of a government role in creating equal social results, declaring rights to education and relief for the unemployed, for example. And these were "rights," not just government help in tough situations that would be provided, if possible. Like today's entitlements, these were deemed rights that citizens could claim against their government. The 1793 French Declaration also contained a strange little article (#27), "Let any person who may usurp the sovereignty be instantly put to death by free men," a right that was exercised liberally during the Reign of Terror that killed 40,000 citizens.

I wouldn't dwell too long on these differences between rights that come from nature and rights that come from government, as if by sticking to the unalienable rights of natural law in their written constitutions, either America or France could have averted the descent into socialism. It would have helped, but it would not have been enough. Certainly both countries confused the issue by expanding their written documents into rights that were already apparent in unalienable rights to life, liberty and property. Adding in, for example, religion, speech and assembly as separate rights, civ as if Locke's basic trio didn't already include them, diluted the unalienable power of the original. And it set us off, as it did France, on an interminable chase of rights, as if any natural right that was not specifically mentioned didn't exist.

It especially didn't help that in their zeal to pile on rights that were clearly not unalienable, such as the equality measures in the second French Declaration and our entitlements today, both countries made it easier to justify redistribution and thus unwind Locke's formula completely, to the point where now in America the cutting edge constitutional experts are arguing over rights to government funded contraception. But as clearly off track as we are now, as far from Locke as we are, I don't believe this was or is the real problem. I don't believe the words in our documents were the reason the doors flew so wide open to socialism in the nineteenth and twentieth centuries, and are flapping in the breeze today.

Given that America and all of the other Western countries in which the tradition of liberty was born are now functionally socialist, regardless of what words they have in their laws and constitutions, it is unlikely that we could have worded our own Constitution sufficiently differently to avoid that result. In order to assess what we might do from here, it will be more productive to get a grip on where we are now. To this end, it may help to look back at how and where we went astray, not with a view to changing some words in our laws or Constitution, or trying to retrace our steps, but with a view to practically assessing the nature of our present dilemma.

Socialism has been the driving Zeitgeist at least since G.W.F. Hegel used that term in the early nineteenth century, mowing down all resistance in its march to dominance. Hegel popularized the dialectic concept, under which history allegedly progresses via a constantly renewing thesis-antithesis-synthesis process, with the synthesis becoming the new thesis, giving rise to a new antithesis, which leads to a new synthesis, and so on. Although Hegel refurbished this theory, he did not invent it, its having been in the basic philosopher's tool kit for some time, including an immediately previous reworking by Jena University professor Johann Fichte, who left Jena in 1799 before Hegel arrived there in 1801. Dialectics came in particularly handy in Hegel's hands, since, like Fichte, his goal as a philosopher was apparently not rigorous analysis, but coming up with a sham theory that implied an inevitability of historical progression so as to justify political action and redistributionist revolution.

The dialectic concept was popular with those looking for justifications to attack wealth and spread it around, and philosophers like Hegel and Fichte were happy to provide it. Originally called "speculation" by Hegel, dialectics was styled as an extension of Kant and worked well to muddy the clear waters the master left behind. It worked to this end because it appeared to have an uncanny, almost scientific ability to predict the future, even to prophesy, which Kant would never have countenanced. It thus meshed in nicely with the messianism of the past that predicted a variety of heaven on earth millennia, and paved the way for Marx, Lenin, the Roosevelts and others to rally the troops around redistribution into the nineteenth and twentieth centuries. Since capitalism was doomed anyway, they seemed to say, we might as well all get on board the socialist train.

There were many flavors of the thesis-antithesis-synthesis theory, but all worked toward the socialist millennium as long as somewhere in the progression they included the collapse of capitalism. Marx's version, dialectical materialism, emphasized class struggle and was later adopted officially by the communists in the Soviet Union. These historical progression models worked so well to attract followers that Hegel was the most popular philosopher in England and America a hundred years after he died, still inspiring leftists like George Bernard Shaw and Herbert Marcuse to devise new ways of popularizing redistribution.

The dialectic model, like Fiore's Third Age theory, has long since faded in terms of its usefulness at implying inevitability. But it paved the way to the incomprehensibility socialism requires, and helped to enable modern redistributionists, like Noam Chomsky, to confuse the faithful further with nonsensical babble calculated to insert religious fervor into their cause. Chomsky has been visibly supportive of the Occupy movement, lending the ragtag campers the gravitas of his intellectual presence, as if their confused message really was righteously, morally superior. A famed philologist and author of over 100 books, the most cited "living scholar" between 1980 and 1992 according to the Arts and Humanities Citation Index, [cv] Chomsky hops between linguistics, other sciences and political philosophy in a manner that implies expertise in all of them. Few can grasp the notoriously impenetrable linguistic field sufficiently to evaluate Chomsky's theories there, but those who can, sound anything but convinced of his infallibility. [cvi] Nonetheless, like Hegel, Chomsky's reputation seems to continually rise on the hopes of his leftist listeners that he is the one, finally, who can put the last nail in capitalism's coffin.

Many of the versions of socialism prophesied by these modern messiahs have gotten so good at confusion that it has become a standard tactic, a reflexive rhetorical dodge to cloak the nonsense in capitalist garb. All of the American presidents who have been identified as socialists, for example, would staunchly deny they are socialists. These would include Woodrow Wilson, Teddy Roosevelt, Franklin Roosevelt, Bill Clinton and Barack Obama, all of which took an oath to defend the Constitution, and then pushed interpretations of law that had undermining the Constitution as their primary objectives. By wrapping their socialism in the flag, by patriotically mentioning freedom, the rule of law and other

American-value-laden terms, and by just being American presidents, these men have managed to deflect the socialist charge that has been leveled at all of them.

Similarly, almost all of the Democrats and Republicans in Congress push with varying degrees of cynicism and innocence laws and rules that can only have redistributionist effects, and are thus clearly more socialist than capitalist, not to mention in all likelihood unconstitutional. And all of them would characterize what they are doing as promoting freedom, the Constitution, and even free market capitalism. These subterfuges, confusions and deceptions are possible because people want them to be true. We all need to believe in the righteousness of our positions, because fighting for these causes is what we do, defining us in our own eyes and in the eyes of others. In America, this means believing in one of the *American* versions of socialism, where nuance and the minor difference between your team's view and the other team's view is all that matters, because that is what the next election will be about, an event in which we are told we have a civic duty, a patriotic obligation to participate. The Blue Team fights to move America from, say, 85% socialist to 86% socialist. The Red Team fights to hold the line at 85%. Meanwhile, both teams maintain a public pretense that the decision is more like between 0% and 100%, a pretense hidden behind code words for socialism or its opposite like "fair" and "change" on the Blue side, or "liberty" and "the Constitution" on the Red side. Both teams pretend the redistribution consequences of the election will be glorious if they win, devastating if they lose, although in reality the difference will be minor and fleeting in any case.

How did we reach a place where the leaders of America are all socialist touts of one stripe or another? Fichte, who was known for attacking Immanuel Kant's rigorous articulation of what can and cannot be proved, may provide the best and earliest example of this pattern in modern times. His arguments are less important than his method, which relied on confusion, beginning with his claim that he was only extending Kant's ideas, rather than attacking them, as Hegel claimed, too, shortly thereafter, also falsely. Fichte's obfuscating style, as well as his playing with those dialectic concepts that were particularly suited to confusion, were picked up by Hegel and others and seem to have initiated a modern tradition that carries to this day in socialist thought. The strategy was to push off from reality to justify action. Truth and reality, such as were articulated in detail by Kant, were like the bars of a prison to these revolutionaries.

Kant described the difference between a phenomenon that can be empirically observed, and a mental image, what he called the "thing in itself" or noumenon. Phenomena can be observed and measured and thereby empirically proved to exist. Things in themselves, i.e., things in the mind only, cannot be empirically observed and measured and, thus, cannot be proved to exist. While certain mathematical statements, or tautologies, may be true a priori, i.e., without observation, the proofs of which could be worked out in and understood by the mind, that fact was not meant to extend the status of a priori truth to any mental images of things or other figments that could not be empirically observed.

Using complex language that sounded to many like Kant, and that Fichte may have deliberately fashioned for that purpose, Fichte averred that Kant's constraints on truth were wrong, that intuitions, especially ones that were agreed on by many, could indeed be true, as if proved by one of Kant's rigorous methods. Schopenhauer captured the effect of Fichte on the debate:

> Fichte, who, because the thing-in-itself had just been discredited, at once prepared a system without any thing-in-itself. Consequently, he rejected the assumption of anything that was not through and through merely our representation, and therefore let the knowing subject be all in all or at any rate produce everything from its own resources. For this purpose, he at once did away with the essential and most meritorious part of Kantian doctrine, the distinction between *a priori* and *a posteriori* and thus between the phenomenon and the thing-in-itself. For he declared everything to be *a priori*, naturally without any evidence for such a monstrous assertion; instead of these, he gave sophisms and even crazy sham demonstrations whose absurdity was concealed under the mask of profundity and of the incomprehensibility ostensibly arising therefrom. Moreover, he appealed boldly and openly to intellectual intuition, that is, really to inspiration. [cvii]

According to various descriptions, Fichte was a "devoted defender of liberty of thought and action and an advocate of political change" who was "stirred by the events and principles of the French Revolution." He was also "considered one of the founders of German nationalism" and was a staunch anti-Semite who wrote *Foundations of Natural Right* in 1796. [cviii] Such fragments, spanning the ideological landscape, give the impression that Fichte was a confusing chameleon, a reputation he apparently fostered and even bragged about to his students.

> In mimicking Kant's difficult style, Fichte produced works that were barely intelligible. "He made no hesitation in pluming himself on his great skill in the shadowy and obscure, by often remarking to his pupils, that 'there was only one man in the world who could fully understand his writings; and even he was often at a loss to seize upon his real meaning.'" [cix]

Philosophically, he was considered a "bridge" between Kant and Hegel. But Fichte has more recently been "appreciated in his own right due to his original insights into the nature of self-consciousness and self-awareness." [cx] One observer offers this earnest attempt to grasp Fichte's meaning:

> The I does this, according to Fichte's analysis, by setting its own limitation, first as only a feeling, then as a sensation, then as an intuition of a thing, and finally as a summons of another person. [cxi]

Remember, this dialectic-sounding progression Fichte posited was happening entirely in the mind. So, unlike Hegel and Marx, who had to reshape historians' views of events that had actually occurred to conform to their dialectic concoctions, and thus had some presumably immutable version of the past to contend with to reach their confusing conclusions, Fichte was operating in the realm of pure imagination. He thus had a free hand to imbue his own subjective theories and views with the seeming imprimatur of universal truth – if only he could rid us of those staid philosophical constraints, like a priori or empirical methods of proof. While Fichte may have been more boastful about his deceptive style than others, he was certainly not alone in promoting the dissolution of reality for political purposes. Marx and Engels openly promoted action over further talk of theory, as do Chomsky and the Occupiers today. Appealing to the mob, the mob to which liberté meant redistribution to accomplish égalité, and the confirming presence of others in the fraternité of the mob, was what Fichte was all about. But that is also what Hegel, who paved the way for Marx, who paved the way for Lenin and the Roosevelts and Chomsky and Obama and all the other revolutionary redistributionists were all about. Appealing to the mob is what they all have always been about.

Given the mass market for mob appreciation in the new democracies, given the thirst for messianic redistributionist prophesies, is it any wonder that unalienable rights began to melt away as soon as these sham philosophers began to tear down the logical edifices built by serious philosophers like Kant and Locke? In fact, isn't it much easier to explain the success of the sham philosophers' philosophies by the demand for them, rather than by attributing that success to their "original insights" or "seminal" status? The original insights of Fiore's Third Age theories or predictions of the Second Coming belong clearly in the realm of religious belief, where Kant would have put them, and where most people, even without Kant's help, now recognize they belong. But the fact that even today, the socialist shamans still enjoy seminal status or similar reverential reputations is evidence of how the West has hoodwinked itself into socialism. It wasn't the shamans who did it. It was We-the-People who demanded it. We extended our reverence for socialism into reverence for the shamans.

Could Locke or Kant have explained their theories more clearly and thus prevented this confusing result? More to the point in our current dilemma: could clearer words in our founding documents have prevented civilization's slide into socialism? While Locke, Kant and Jefferson would undoubtedly have admitted that there is always room for improvement in phraseology, it seems certain that no mere words could have prevented this red tide, this blood-dimmed tide, from eventually swamping their good works.

Did freedom mean unalienable rights protected by government? Or did freedom mean the right to free help from government? This question was in play at least since the American and French revolutions. Our Declaration of Independence went with the first formulation. But by the time our Constitution was ratified in 1788, the first formulation was already giving ground to the second, a process Jefferson himself may have been lamenting when he wrote from Paris that very year, "the natural progress of things is for liberty to yield and government to gain ground." [cxii] In any event, by the time of the second French Declaration of the Rights of Man and Citizen in 1793, the second formulation was firmly in control.

The United States was fortunate, however. Perhaps it was our isolation in the New World, or the relative newness of our society, or having gone first through the revolutionary door. In any case, somehow the United States went for a full century run under the first formulation before the second began to seriously unwind it. As a result, we did something unequaled before or since. From a standing start, we created far more wealth than any individuals or any society had ever created in such a short time, or for that matter in any span of time. The individuals who created their own and society's wealth often started poor and unconnected to any traditional sources of power or money. But in just a few decades they created wealth for themselves that broke the historical record and has not been equaled since. And it wasn't just one or two lucky one-offs. The whole Robber Baron cohort created more wealth and better organization for the society in which they operated than had ever existed before, and provided the industrial foundation for the strongest, wealthiest, most innovative society in world history. And it did these things almost overnight from almost nothing.

Sadly, since at least the passage of the Sherman Antitrust Act of 1890, the first formulation of freedom based on property rights has been giving ground to the second one based on redistribution. How does Sherman fit in with the shamans? Like a glove. The underlying theories are so conflicted and confusing and nonsensical that adherence to them belongs, like Fiore's Third Age prophesies, in the realm of religion. In a disingenuous dance that Fichte would have reveled in, antitrust socialism has even managed, in Bork's phrase mentioned before, to gain a reputation as "a law that became, and for a long time remained, the politically potent symbol of the virtues of free and unregulated markets." [cxiii] But so ensconced in their lucrative and powerful roles are today's antitrust shamans that they constitute a power elite similar to the combination of church and state that ran the Inquisition in the Middle Ages. The antitrust agencies are the jewels in the crown of oppression that is today preventing property rights from working their wealth-creating wonders.

While many have written on where antitrust went wrong, the core problem lies not in poor choices or incorrect application of an otherwise good idea, as most of its critics allege. The core problem is far more fundamental than that. Antitrust was a bad idea from the very beginning. Its core problem lies with the prevention of natural rights under natural law that the first formulation of Americans' rights was meant to guarantee, the one in our Declaration of Independence. That socialism under the second formulation, the formulation of the French Revolution, is now ascendant is the issue that, practically speaking, we will have to grapple with if we want to restore America's promise. Unfortunately, it will not be so easy as going back to the Constitution, as often called for, or even strict construction of the Constitution's words. If the people want socialism under the second formulation, if they want the "right" to free goods redistributed from others, if that is what they think freedom means, there is no realistic hope that the Constitution can save us from it now.

There may, however, be a more practical way of getting at the problem. The 2012 political season has already produced a variety of proposals to eliminate government departments and agencies, perhaps all unrealistically impractical, too, but nonetheless on the table for public consideration. Even President Obama is talking about combining a few, while various Republicans have talked of eliminating up to five. Such proposals almost never go anywhere. Eliminating the Department of Education, for example, which is a noted downward redistribution vehicle beloved of teachers' unions, is very high-hanging fruit. But since the idea of eliminating agencies is in play anyway, and occasionally discussed by both parties, if targets are picked carefully there may be a chance now to actually get it done.

Antitrust and intellectual property agencies, which are the primary bastions of modern socialism and thus doing much harm to America, are also among the least understood agencies. For our purposes, this is good. It means that they are also among the least protected and most vulnerable to elimination. Disposing entirely of them might be more possible than we think, because of two factors: number one, the lack of public understanding of what they do, and number two, their total lack of value.

The SEC, in particular, is low-hanging fruit. Eliminating it would affect lawyers, lobbyists, bureaucrats and others whose actions and rationales never have been understood by the public, but no one else. The public does not perceive itself as having a recognizable stake in any of the activities of the SEC. The rationales behind the Commission's market structure reforms are confused, unsupportable and perceived as ineffective by a public that does not understand them or recognize how it benefits from them. Although the Commission often references redistributionist or big-is-bad causes, the structures and means by which the Commission allegedly achieves its goals are at best bewildering. Even the attacks on inside traders and big dealers over the years, while springing from a populist bent, are little understood and often disagreed with in their effects. And there are the frequent scandals attributable to the SEC, like the Madoff Ponzi scheme and the Flash Crash, both of which, in spite of the Commission's protestations and cover-ups, the public correctly blames on the SEC.

Then there is the accumulating and accelerating series of black swan events that keep on happening even as the SEC ratchets up its responses to them: the Flash Crash, the Bats IPO, the Facebook IPO, the Knightmare on Wall Street. Every problem is presented as a compliance error, as if some big bad rich guys didn't do what they were supposed to do, as if BATS or Nasdaq or Knight could have tested their systems well enough to prevent the debacles they are now associated with. [cxiv] Nowhere is it acknowledged that under the high frequency regime, it is impossible to prevent these things with testing because laboratory tests won't find the bugs and real life tests are impossible to arrange. Since it was the SEC that created this high frequency monster, in which testing is practically speaking impossible, its public criticism of BATS and Nasdaq and Knight for being lax in testing and perhaps out of compliance with SEC rules is disingenuous at best.

What would happen if the SEC were eliminated? Is there something in its ongoing operations that would be missed? Yes, but only in a positive sense. The markets could again learn to raise capital effectively, as they did before the SEC set out to reform them. And investors could again assume they are sentient adults that can decide on their own whether to invest in a new company or not. Most important, the markets themselves could work out again through normal competition how to structure themselves without the pernicious presence of the SEC trying to create roles for itself. This is not far fetched. The SEC did not exist at all in 1933, and its National Market System did not exist in 1974. There is no evidence that our markets have been made more effective by SEC action since these dates, and lots of evidence that they have been made much worse because of the SEC.

The belief that the SEC is needed in order to make us confident enough to invest is nonsense. Further, in the degree to which it is believed to be true and we are confident of the SEC's ability to fulfill this mission, it is a bad thing, not a good thing. Such confidence is the very reason so many investors behave foolishly and naïvely, putting their money into schemes and scams of all kinds believing the SEC has their back, as so many of the victims of the Madoff Ponzi scheme did. Merely removing the SEC from all of its ineffective maneuvering in this pointless and counterproductive role would restore the healthy skepticism that investors would otherwise naturally have. They would again understand and live according to the old maxim that, when something sounds too good to be true, it probably is.

In addition, in the absence of government roles to create investor protection and fairness, it is a competitive necessity of brokers, dealers and exchanges to provide these features and they do, both in order to survive and in order to thrive versus their peers. Investors who feel unsafe or unfairly treated will not use the facilities that make them feel that way, so markets have no choice but to compete at providing safety and fairness. But once government takes over these functions, the motivations run in reverse. It becomes a competitive necessity to do as little as possible to comply with SEC rules, to leave surveillance, enforcement, and market structure to the cops rather than the Darwinian marketplace. Natural ethics enforcement mechanisms like Dictum Meum Pactum, which discovers and banishes bad actors and dishonesty from the industry, are dropped as anachronistic throwbacks that waste time and money. And innovation is pointless under the clone-based market structure competition of high frequency trading where only speed matters. Getting rid of the SEC would allow all of these problems to repair themselves naturally as antitrust-based fragmentation disappeared and markets again became centralized, focused and understandable.

It won't be easy to take down this much government. The SEC employs 4,000 bureaucrats, and the industry lawyers and other elites that deal in their processes are legion. But eliminating the Commission would not require nearly the courage, insight and determination our first Revolution required. It would not require Patriots to pledge their lives, their fortunes and their sacred honor, as the Founders did when they signed the Declaration of Independence. But it would reboot America economically and instantly stop the damage antitrust is doing to our capital markets and standard of living, giving us time and resources to work out what we really believe about foreign wars and redistribution before it is too late.

9. The American People

Red State, Blue State; Republican, Democrat; conservative, liberal; right, left; capitalist, socialist; Tea Party, Occupy; Wall Street Journal, New York Times; Fox, CNN; Hannity, Colmes; Matalin, Carville; George Will, George Stephanopoulos. For the CNBC cognoscenti: Rick Santelli, Steve Liesman; Joe Kernen, Adam Ross Sorkin; Michelle Caruso-Cabrera, Becky Quick; Larry Kudlow, Jim Cramer. Everyone identifies with either the Red Team or the Blue Team and can be counted on to debate from their team's perspective, even when just reporting the news. Although redistribution is not always explicitly visible, it usually is, and is never far away. In any case, the other issues tend strongly to divide the debaters into the same Red and Blue camps, as if they too were about redistribution.

The debates ostensibly seek to discern what attitudes our society should have about the issues, both separately and collectively, and what we should do about them through government policy. A habit of the debates, a virtual protocol, is to tear one's hair out over the inroads of the other team, which are alleged to be perverting the purpose and character of America. Half of America thinks the country is going off a cliff because of the perversions of the Red Team. The other half thinks we're going off the cliff because of the perversions of the Blue Team. Since almost everyone thinks we're going off a cliff for one reason or another, almost everyone thinks we're on the wrong track, and is angry about it.

While the Red Team wants to go back to America's constitutional roots, and the Blue Team places America's roots in the alleged fairness of Constitution-shredding traditions like the New Deal, the reality is these are both tropes, flourishes that shape an argument of the moment for either upward or downward redistribution. Like other seemingly unrelated issues – cultural, moral, religious, defense, etc. – the argument over whether America's true character lies in fairness or the Constitution is so remote practically speaking from the redistribution levers under debate, that it serves, as these other issues do, only as a marker of tribal loyalties and team allegiance designed to provoke emotion, righteous anger, action. Depending on how these settle into voters' minds, the majority of the moment will either swing redistribution upwards or downwards, but generally not by much or for long. The momentary cheering on one side and hair pulling out on the other will only set the stage for further rounds of the same argument.

Why can't the debate be settled? Why can't we find the true consensus of America? The reason is that the payers of redistribution will always say the amount is too large, while the receivers will always say it is too small, *no matter what the amount is*. Every argument for greater or lesser progressivity in the tax code, for example, will continue after an election and after any legislated change in progressivity resulting from the election. Even if the ballyhooed Simpson-Bowles compromise were to be adopted, not a single one of the issues causing the fiscal crisis would have been resolved. Everyone on both the Red Team and the Blue Team would simply adjust and press for further advantage or defend against further inroads from wherever the last round left things.

As impossible as consensus is on redistribution, it is if anything even more remote on the other issues. In fact, the emotions in the culture wars, the religion wars, the civil rights wars, the education wars, the abortion wars, the marriage and family wars, the defense wars – even the Constitution wars – will always be out of control. Not only are there no natural guides to where the answers lie, these are the issues most likely to excite deep hell-or-high-water anger and violence. They engender easy self-identification with the group you belong to as a matter of faith, tradition, upbringing, race, class, sex, sexual preference or other clear divisions.

More important, self-identification in these fields is as much a matter of who you are *not* as of who you are. This makes it easy to justify policies that harm the other side. You know who they are, and they are not you. You don't look like them, act like them, think like them. So maybe they really aren't human, after all. The Occupy protesters behind the sign, "Talk About My Ideas, Not My Hygiene" stare at the well-dressed commuters walking by, who occasionally glance over at them. Neither is interested in the other's ideas. Each sees the other as a threat to his personal economic health, as well as the economic health of the nation. Probably more importantly in terms of the intensity of their emotions is that each sees the other as someone who harbors improper or immoral attitudes on many non-economic issues, too, and is therefore undeserving of sympathy or concern.

Meanwhile, the redistribution arguments become more and more intractable. When property is up for debate, there is no such thing as a correct tax rate, a correct minimum wage, a correct pension payment, a correct retirement age, a correct COLA formula, or a correct anything. Worse, in a plural society, there is no correct answer to any of the cultural, religious or moral issues, either. But the implicit premise of the debate is that a single answer must be found that is good for the whole society, one that government can impose on everyone, a universal truth, good for this country and the world.

And the answer must be applicable to all the issues in a consistent way. It would not do to take a Blue Team answer for one issue, a Red Team answer for the next one, a Blue Team answer next, and so on. That would be unacceptable to both teams. That is why Simpson-Bowles is unacceptable, although it is only dealing with relatively simpler issues of fiscal consequence. But even if in the direst fiscal crisis it did manage to pass, that would still not resolve anything in the fiscal realm, much less in the wider realms of culture, religion or morality. For all of these realms, the underlying assumption of the debates is that either the Blue Team's whole platform or the Red Team's whole platform must be chosen.

America's original religious freedom and property rights worked because they settled all issues of distribution and culture naturally in ways that accommodated different choices and results. But those guarantees are long gone. Now every contentious issue is said to be in need of a national conversation to figure out what the policy should be for everyone. No longer free to choose as individuals, we are bound by either Red Team or Blue Team positions, and are exhorted to participate in that national conversation through our parties and votes. While there is some jostling within each party over priorities and emphasis before a platform is settled on, the assumption remains that no Blue platform could ever satisfy a Red

Team member, and no Red platform could ever satisfy a Blue Team member. So the only question is, which side are you on?

The debates cannot be settled, ever. But that doesn't mean they stand still. The more they fester in an unsettled condition, the more both sides get self-righteous, indignant, divisive and personal. And the angrier they become, the more they cry out for a powerful, all-knowing government to take control. But since government is nothing but a reflection and embodiment of the debates, it cannot find solutions any more than the debaters can. Government can, however, camouflage its impotence at finding consensus with ever-greater power to impose its will.

Hitler sought Lebensraum to the east of Germany, first on behalf of the German people living in Germany, and then on behalf of ethnic Germans wherever they lived, and finally would have gone for global domination to impose Nazi industrial and social policies on everyone, including eugenic genetic policies to assure Aryan purity. Had his visions in the *Second Book* of *Mein Kampf* come to pass, they would have constituted a unified theory of government for the world, covering all things for all people everywhere. It seems so obvious looking back that it was a bad policy that could only come to a bad end. But such things are never so obvious midstream. One reason it was not obvious to Germans, or at least could not be mentioned out loud if it was, was that speaking up meant stunted careers, ostracism, intimidation, and death.

Political correctness is our equivalent of that policy in its intermediate stages. The American people today are cowering in their kitchens, afraid to even mention certain categories in the presence of family or friends, much less colleagues, for fear of appearing to harbor politically incorrect thoughts. Thoughts, for example, that it is not right to promote people because of their race or sex, or to punish someone extra harshly for what was in his mind when he committed a "hate crime." This policy obviously dilutes the protection the law provides against actual, non-hate crimes. But all of these diversity policies have a much worse effect, too, one that causes the cowering and ultimately drives toward a "final solution." [cxv]

Punishing people for what is supposedly in their minds is the essence of evil. It has already led to a culture of division by sex, race, class and other groupings that blocks the careers of those who do not visibly support diversity, or cheer its depredations, or whose groups are at the bottom of the politically correct pile, such as lower class white men are in America today. Everyone says Promote Me Because My Group Is More Entitled Than Yours, even lower class white men who are sick and tired of being overstepped by affirmative actions promoting other groups. Such strategies sharpen divisions, destroy the livelihoods of those in the losing groups, and raise desires for revenge. Demagogues exploit the anger and denunciations such situations provoke, as Hitler did when he accused Jews of thinking what he had been thinking, namely starting World War II and taking over the world:

> If the international Jewish financiers outside Europe should succeed in plunging the nations once more into a world war, then the result will not be the bolshevization of the earth, and thus the victory of Jewry, but the annihilation of the Jewish race in Europe. [cxvi]

Jewish bankers had long been the assumed cause of German problems, assumed, that is, according to the politically correct views of their time. Anti-Semites like Fichte in the 18th and 19th centuries promoted anti-Semitic nationalism and sought to prevent Jews from becoming German citizens. "In regards to Jews getting 'civil rights,' [Fichte] argued that this would only be possible if one managed 'to cut off all their heads in one night, and to set new ones on their shoulders that should contain not a single Jewish idea.'" [cxvii]

In the 20th century versions of such thinking, Hitler and others accused the conspiring financiers of, among other things: undermining the war effort at home during World War I by causing strikes in munitions factories; a "stab-in-the-back" by urging surrender when the Germans were winning in the field; [cxviii] and concocting with foreign powers the economically crippling reparations payments of the Weimar Treaty. Given all these things the Jewish financiers had allegedly conspired on to harm Germans, it may not have sounded like such a stretch to Hitler's audience that they were also planning to start World War II and take over the world.

We may think today, with the distance of history and knowing what happened afterward, that we modern Americans are not to be swayed by such paranoid fears. But we are. Political correctness gives us all the scope we need to impute thought crimes to others. And to the regime-of-mind inquisitor, everyone is guilty until proven innocent, which is never. Thus as a society, we assume the rich are guilty of greed, men are guilty of sexism, whites are guilty of racism, heterosexuals are guilty of hating homosexuals, and that there are many other ongoing thought crimes in need of restitution and punishment.

The regime of mind requires not noticing or complaining when restitution requires giving advantages to some groups over other groups via special civil rights or affirmative actions. The regime of mind requires not mentioning that affirmative action is official, government-sanctioned discrimination, and that there is no conceivable construction of either the Constitution or the Declaration of Independence that would allow it. If it occurs to you that Hitler's policies – up to and including the Holocaust – amounted to affirmative action for Aryans, the regime of mind requires that you keep it to yourself.

The regime of mind requires that we ignore the genocide unfolding in South Africa against whites under the democracy we urged on that country, [cxix] and it requires not noticing that, when our politically correct media embrace former President Clinton and others celebrating Nelson Mandela's 94th birthday, they are embracing the icon of a budding evil similar to Hitler's that may yet expand into something just as ugly, or worse. Evil as Hitler was, at least his policies promoting Aryans were not endorsed by the United States, the United Nations and "the world."

The regime of mind required us to look away as Hutus murdered Tutsis in Rwanda, to forget about that "never again" thing, to even avoid calling it what it obviously was, genocide, in order to get out of our legal obligation to stop it. [cxx] Like Jews in Hitler's Germany, Tutsis had once been the market dominant minority in Rwanda and were conspiring to return, according to government propaganda. So why wouldn't the Hutus feel entitled under our theories of democratic egalitarian pluralism to murder Tutsis? Why wouldn't they assume that equality of results is the only legitimate outcome of democracy and, therefore, feel entitled to take revenge against the privileged minority Tutsis? The regime of mind requires that we sweep such episodes under the rug, that we never consider our hand in causing them, and that we not notice when the atrocity-versus-atrocity pattern seems to emerge wherever we encourage or assist those long-seething majorities to assert their democratic rights: Rwanda, Serbia, Iraq, Libya, Syria.

The fear of American politicians and people, generally, to speak up about such things is the rough equivalent of the timidity of Germans that allowed the Holocaust to occur under their noses. The regime of mind requires not noticing or remembering Hitler's 1939 speech quoted above, which, by putting Jews at the center of an international conspiracy of rich bankers, put them in the same place as the hated bankers of today. Jews were the 1% of that time and the Nazis were the 99%.

A propaganda film, *Der Ewige Jude,* (The Eternal Jew) produced by Joseph Goebbels at Hitler's request, put the Jewish conspiracy at the top of German society and income in Berlin. According to the film, Jews were only 0.2% of common laborers, but were 15% of prosecutors, 23% of judges, 52% of doctors, 60% of lawyers, and had over 12 times the wealth of the average German (10,000 marks versus 810 marks). Such inequality, according to Hitler and Goebbels, needed to be addressed by government.

The mental crimes the 1%ers are being convicted of in the court of public opinion today aren't much different from those underlying the supposed international Jewish banking conspiracy of Hitler's time. While anti-Semitism is not a component of today's jealousy of the rich, at least not officially, we should temper our relief. Amy Chua's thesis, in which market dominant minorities are targeted for revenge by majorities due to democratization and globalization is morphing today into a general case for revenge against successful people everywhere by less successful people anywhere. And since there are often easily recognized racial and ethnic markers identifying the dominant group, the potential for racial conflict is always just one step away in the class wars. The regime of mind requires not noticing that racial animosity is fostered by the class wars, and is powerfully supercharged by any and all claims that "this is how democracy is supposed to work."

The regime of mind requires not noticing that it is absurd to prevent police from profiling. This means that we either have to do with much less protection for the same amount of money, or spend much more money to get the same amount of protection. And it means that, although we are vulnerable to losing thousands of lives as we lose a city, we have to try to prevent such an attack without using our most valuable tool to expose it before it is too late. And why do we do this? We do it because we have convinced ourselves we have a "civil right" to not be profiled. This is nonsense. Under natural law, we not only do not have any such right, but the opposite is true: we have a right to discriminate on any basis we choose, including on prejudice or using profiling. It is the ultimate in government mind control to attempt to wipe out these natural and beneficial mental functions in the interest of political correctness.

Not only should we be able to discriminate individually, we have a right to have our police and other security professionals protect us from harm using whatever means are most efficient and effective, including profiling. If, *in the opinion of police,* stop-and-frisk prevents crime efficiently or, *in the opinion of airline security,* profiling young male Arabs from Muslim countries efficiently finds potential hijackers or, *in the opinion of the military,* homosexuals or women should not be freely included in our fighting forces, it is suicidal of our society to block their judgments in the interest of diversity. We have effectively turned every institution in our society, at all levels of government, military services, police departments, fire departments, education institutions, businesses, etc., into petri dishes where we subordinate whatever their original purposes were to a new mission of being showcases for tolerance and inclusion. It is politically incorrect to mention that this policy is demeaning to the dignity of its alleged beneficiaries, because it presumes they could not make it on their own. And it is forbidden to mention that the previous missions of the institutions that have been co-opted for the purpose of creating diversity propaganda might have been compromised.

If we were honest, we would acknowledge that the anti-profiling agenda is nothing but downward redistribution in a different guise, designed around the presumed imperative of promoting the rise of allegedly aggrieved groups by giving them special advantages. Something very close to this politically correct picture was part of the official narrative of socialists like Marx and Kropotkin, who celebrated not just the deserving poor story, but also the all-knowing poor story, as if the world would run more efficiently if the meek did in fact inherit the earth.

The politically correct subtext extends forcefully into our actual lives, requiring adherence to its dictates in our attitudes and demeanor as a condition of employment or advancement in our jobs, and in order to participate in the other social engagements of life, including marriage and family. Everyone shrinks from honestly acknowledging what is going on, because candor would stunt or kill our prospects in any social endeavor. So we look away; we look down; we keep quiet.

The American people of 1776 were made of sterner stuff. Led from the front by Patriots willing to pledge, *and literally risk*, their fortunes and their lives for the cause of freedom, their sacred honor would never have permitted them to participate in the dishonest dissembling that is de rigueur today.

10. The Pursuit of Happiness

Government today increasingly means global government. The assumption is that through the same kind of Red Team versus Blue Team debate we have in the United States, global government can also figure out how to produce wealth efficiently and distribute it fairly. "Redistributionism" has become the functional equivalent of a state religion that mandates all of the politically correct attitudes and policies described in the previous chapter, and does so on a global basis. It allows no separation between Church and State, because Redistributionism is a moral code that *requires* implementation *by* the state. Heretics that refuse to follow its dictates are denied their right to pursue happiness or worse. Renegade nations are targeted for regime change through sanctions or war.

Back home in the United States, as if to show support for our troops abroad, all parties support either the Red Team or the Blue Team version of Redistributionism. It has no official name, of course. Redistributionism is only a pejorative stand-in; Political Correctism would do nearly as well. Believers would use more flattering terms, words like "democratic," "fair," "balanced," "progressive," even "global," "multi-cultural" or, in some ardent quarters, "socialist" might find favor. How about, The Peoples Progressive Republic of Democratic Pluralism? It wouldn't matter. Redistributionism would still be the functionally correct term for the PPRDP.

What became the Nazi Party was a name that began as the Marxist-sounding German Workers Party, the DAP. [cxxi] Then its leaders, including Adolf Hitler, thought it would sound even more appealing if words referencing nationalism and socialism were added, since each of these concepts was independently popular. So they called their party the National Socialist German Workers Party, the NSDAP. [cxxii] In the end the abbreviation for the first syllable of the first word and the second syllable of the second word stuck, and "Nazi" was the name remembered by history. Under any name, there is no mistaking the zeal of believers in these state religions who do everything in their power to snuff out heretical challenges to government prerogative. The formal name for this kind of all-controlling, unitary government is "fascism." And just as Mussolini's version was said to unify the right and left, America's version today subsumes both the Red Team and the Blue Team in their Redistributionism kabuki dance.

Occasionally, challenges to the official faith pop up. The conflict over taxpayer-funded contraception, for example, or whether religious institutions can be required to provide it, not to mention the spats over where and when Christmas carols can be sung, demonstrate discomfort with where Redistributionism is taking us. But while these episodes pose as freedom-of-religion problems, as if suppressing all traditional faiths equally meant freedom, their invariable settlements in favor of the state are in reality obliterating freedom of religion in order to establish Redistributionism as the state religion.

While such controversies point to something radically wrong with our freedoms, including our presumed freedom of religion, they have not broached yet the fundamental source of the problem, which lies in the suppression of our right to the pursuit of happiness. Attempting to guarantee freedom of religion as a separate right in the Bill of Rights was a mistake. We would have done better with John Locke's original "life, liberty and property" formula, or with Thomas Jefferson's restatement of it as "life, liberty and the pursuit of happiness," both of which naturally included freedom of religion and would have protected it from the political correctness attacks that are undermining it today. By separately guaranteeing religious freedom in the Bill of Rights, we opened the door to its elimination.

It is not known for sure why Thomas Jefferson substituted "pursuit of happiness" for "property" in the familiar John Locke trio. One theory is that "pursuit of happiness" was a more ringing phrase and thus had greater potential to rally political support, which, given the contentious arguments at the time, may indeed have been a consideration. The phrase itself was not unknown to Locke and others, and certainly captures the essence of an unalienable right of human action once the rights to life and liberty are secured. Further, since that right of human action would often be directed at the accumulation of property, it was not unreasonable to make the substitution, even if the right to property were its only purpose. But while the right to the pursuit of happiness included the right to accumulate and keep property, it also included the right to pursue happiness for other purposes, too, including the right of assembly and association generally, which would have included the rights to freedom of religion and others in the Bill of Rights.

Looking at the property angle first, one need go no further to see how far we have come from having a right to the pursuit of happiness than to contemplate minimum wage laws. Here both employee and employer are blocked from pursuing happiness unless their agreement conforms to government's constraints. But minimum wage laws are only the tip of the iceberg in terms of blocking our pursuit of happiness. All attempts to create equality of results, from equal pay for equal work to the Community Reinvestment Act abridge the rights of people to pursue happiness and, in so doing, hinder the right of freedom of association which is its essential element. What these egalitarian measures accomplish in the employment arena, for example, is to create better-paying jobs for a few at the expense of the many who can't get jobs at all in the stunted labor market at its artificially higher mandated price. They also deny the right of employers to pursue happiness by expanding their businesses, which would create even more jobs. While the claimed value of minimum wage laws is fairness, which some call a right to a living wage, this is in reality just another entitlement aimed at egalitarian redistribution. Its effect, like all such entitlements, is to deny the right to pursue happiness to others. But such phony rights are holy writ in Redistributionism, the state religion for which we have thrown away our unalienable right to the pursuit of happiness.

Under natural law, the unhindered right to form associations with other people, individually and in groups, is the most essential freedom we have – or had. It is the essence of what enables us to pursue happiness. Whether we do so for commercial purposes, for religious purposes, for social purposes, or for any other purposes, a free people would not abridge the right to freedom of association. There is, therefore, no more clear indication that we are no longer free than that government presumes, both through law, and through the politically correct attitudes that have built up around law, to take away our right to freedom of association.

Freedom of association means the right to exercise our powers of discrimination as we see fit, to seek out good associations and avoid bad ones. And yes, that would include the right to be prejudiced or bigoted. In order to be free, we must be able to choose, for any reason, to make or not make associations. A free people could choose to associate only with men, or only with women, or only with rich people, or only with poor people. Free people could allow onto their property, including restaurants or apartments for rent or businesses they own, only black people, or only white people, all people except for certain named people, or only certain named people and no one else. Free people could associate only with prejudiced people, or only with non-prejudiced people, and could use any method of their choosing to make the determination, including entirely random coin flips or their own mood swings.

Visitors, patrons, renters and employees could make their own decisions as well. They could decide, both individually and in joint actions such as boycotts, to visit, patronize, rent from or work for only those persons or establishments that let certain groups in, or only those that use coin flips or mood swings to make the call. They could also avoid establishments that use such prejudiced or silly methods, and tell all of their friends to do the same. They could use their own powers of discrimination to discriminate against those who discriminate on objectionable bases, such as racial prejudice, or that fail to discriminate on positive bases, such as honesty, integrity, good manners or other forms of merit. They could use their own moral compasses or commercial insights to make such judgments, and could choose to associate only with others who reach similar conclusions.

Private universities (and a free people would not have any other kind, since government support or subsidies is a form of redistribution) would be free to admit only men or only women. They could preferentially admit or deny admission to any persons or types of persons they choose to, for any reason, including race, gender, sexual preference, political party, religious affiliation or athletic skills, or seek to maintain any ratio of their choosing between them.

Individuals could form unions and agree to work only for employers that only hire union members. Employers could choose to hire only union employees or to hire only non-union employees or any mix of their choosing between them.

Owners of property and businesses could set the prices and terms of sale of their property to other people as they see fit. They could agree to cooperate with others in setting prices, and could sell at different prices to different people if they want to.

Securities dealers and traders could form membership associations that bar participation in buying and selling securities created by them to non-members. They could call these associations "stock exchanges." Such stock exchanges could fix commissions, spreads and other terms of participation governing their members as they see fit. They could bar their members from participating in other exchanges or otherwise dealing with members of other exchanges. They could also agree to not compete with other exchanges.

By arrogating unto itself the right to make all fundamental decisions of discrimination for us, our government has blocked the main means by which we humans improve our condition, including by making moral judgments that guide our associations. There is no evidence or reason to think that government can make such judgments on our behalf better than we could on our own. Our society is not more efficient because of it. And it is certainly not more moral because of it, as the peoples of Nazi Germany and Soviet Russia discovered.

If you comb through the choices government has made for us, you will find that every decision has been made as if its sole purpose were to make government bigger. Every intervention is by definition bigger, of course. But the failures and debacles that result from intervention always lead to more and bigger interventions and worse problems and bigger failures down the road. The housing policies of the Community Reinvestment Act led to over-investment in housing and the real estate crash and Great Recession. The National Market System, where government took over the operation of the stock market, led to the IPO bust and contributed to the subsequent rise in the unemployment rate and increase in extended unemployment benefit payments and expanded deficits. The "Wars" on Poverty, Inflation, Drugs and Terrorism only seemed to produce more of what they were warring against and led to a plethora of negative unintended consequences, all of which became excuses for even greater government involvement subsequently.

These examples point to a pattern in which whatever choice government makes is designed to make government bigger and more powerful as it removes our unalienable rights. Such reliance on government blocks the natural formation of wealth-creating networks and destroys their ability to distribute wealth fairly according to natural property rights. The only possible consequence is an angry and divided society that looks to government for solutions to the problems government is causing, with each faction and division demanding larger and larger shares of the inevitably shrinking pie.

What would happen if we were again free to pursue happiness, including in politically incorrect ways, such as those described above? Would we go back to Jim Crow? Slavery? Would subjugation of women re-emerge? Would the upward progress of women and minorities cease? Scientifically speaking, preferential attachment is what we're talking about when we say "pursuit of happiness." It is the unhindered right to form or decline to form social, commercial and other types of associations or attachments that drive the evolution of society as increasingly sophisticated and complex networks form. Such evolution naturally creates modes of interaction that are conflict free because they are freely chosen, which is especially important when resources are scarce.

Such natural evolution under freedom of association also leads to the formation of ever more efficient networks for supplying and distributing resources, leading to progressive relief from the scarcities that caused conflict in the first place. [cxxiii] Equally important, the more efficient networks are more satisfying in terms of employment opportunities for everyone involved in them. As discussed in chapter 7, natural evolution leads to better options for both the weak and the strong, for bosses and labor, for masters and slaves, for men and women, which options naturally and progressively resolve the conflicts between these groups. Dominance and coercion give way to voluntary and increasingly attractive means for all parties to get what they want, such as larger and richer enterprises for the owners and bosses, and more attractive and varied employment opportunities for labor. Just as brutal ancient institutions, like slavery and the abuse of women, were largely competed away by institutions that provided more attractive options for both brutalizers and brutalized, all along the way at every stage of civilization's advance, the subjugation and exploitation of the past is competed away as more attractive institutions for the strong emerge that leave the coercive institutions behind.

For all of these reasons, economic improvement due to network formation, and the consequent relief from conflicts over resources, are the primary reasons for improvements that are usually, but incorrectly, attributed to civil rights. In the degree to which freedom is allowed to improve both economic conditions and the relations between the weak and the strong, the position of women and minorities will continue to improve. In the degree to which lack of freedom continues to hamper our economy and block natural progress in relations, the position of women and minorities will fail to improve or deteriorate. Civil rights have almost nothing to do with it. It is when governments arrest the processes of economic and social evolution that problems arise, not when the natural processes are free to work their wonders.

One of those wonders is the tendency of preferential attachment, or rich get richer, to lead to a wide divergence in levels of wealth and incomes. An environment with a wide spread of wealth and incomes is an environment in which all people can find employment, regardless of their diverse skills, backgrounds, preferences and other differentiating characteristics. Inequality is not, as the politically correct pundits tell us, a bad thing. In fact, if we weren't so preoccupied with envy, we would find that inequality is a very good thing, at least in terms of employment and consequent happiness. The more inequality there is, the easier it is for everyone to find productive, satisfying, lucrative work with prospects for improvement. Inequality is both a cause of and an effect of a wide divergence in types of employment, as well as in the kinds, manners and amounts of compensation, both for all tasks and for any particular task. This is the very condition that would maximize employment opportunities.

Think of it as the opposite of the Marxist formula, where everyone is given whatever he needs, regardless of what he produces. If society is required to stick to this formula, then employers – even those working for the state – face a dilemma. Since they cannot pay for performance, from a work incentive standpoint, it is as if there is a single wage that employers are required to pay. Employers would be able to hire in this circumstance only those few who produce exactly the value to the employer of the mandated wage. Employees that are worth more would not work (unless they were forced to, as slaves), and the employer would not hire those that were worth less (except out of Marxist patriotism or pity, perhaps). Thus work would happen only on those few tasks – or perhaps only that one task – that have the same value to the employer as the amount he is mandated to pay.

So at opposite ends of the spectrum, there is the perfect equality of one-wage Marxism, which at the extreme would hire only one person in the whole society, while at the other end is wide inequality allowing for the maximizing of employment by providing something for everyone to do. Equal pay for equal work may sound appealing and fair, but if one thinks about it a little longer, it becomes obvious that the downside is that the policy blocks employment that, for whatever reason, could have been contracted at unequal pay, but wasn't. This means that both the employees that could have been hired and the employers that would have hired them have had their rights to the pursuit of happiness blocked by the equal-pay policy. And the whole society has lost out on the additional production, growth and tax revenues that their employment would have engendered.

The value of natural inequality goes beyond maximizing employment, as important in its own right as that is. What inequality also does is allow the evolution of social structures past the primitive stages where fights over resources led to brutal institutions like slavery, the abuse of women, and other exploitation of the weak by the strong. Such evolution involves the naturally coordinated interleaving of many different kinds of networks: economic, social, religious, political and others. It is through such natural evolution, and only through such natural evolution, that the good things societies can do are made possible and evils are avoided.

Slavery and serfdom largely fell away due to distastes for the practice that arose in several societies, including our own in the nineteenth century. Our Civil War was an unnecessary and very painful aberration in this regard, according to Thomas DiLorenzo in *The New Lincoln*.

> Why didn't Lincoln do what much of the rest of the world did in the nineteenth century and end slavery peacefully through compensated emancipation? Between 1800 and 1860, dozens of countries, including the entire British Empire, ended slavery peacefully; only in the United States was a war involved. [cxxiv]

And slavery itself was probably an improvement over the previous alternative treatment when a savage society conquered another. Such distastes are examples of the operation of preferential attachment leading to the formation of networks that eschew ugly practices like slavery or the take-no-prisoners slaughters that preceded it. Through the strength of superior models, whether moral, commercial or other, the new models overcame earlier models that relied on slaves and serfs, which had overcome still earlier models that slaughtered conquered peoples. Experts did not create these models in conference rooms. The more humane and more efficient models were all the result of natural network formation, undirected by government or experts. Chivalry, "a readiness to help the weak," [cxxv] was a core moral precept of the society that became the British Empire and the wealthiest in the world. Yet chivalry was not thought up by experts or legislated by government. Nor was the common law, nor the natural law in which the Founders of America believed.

We should never forget that all of the great evils in history, from witch-hunts to death camps, were products of government. They were not products of common law, or natural law, or preferential attachment, or the pursuit of happiness. It is when government gets out of control, when it breaks out of the constraints that a decent society places on it, that things go wrong. However imperfect the Founders'

Constitution was, they at least attempted to give us the right to pursue happiness as the best protection they could think of against runaway government. It is sad and a potential tragedy in the making that we have walked away from the Constitution they worked so hard and fought so bravely to give us. But it isn't worth the air to speculate on whether modern Americans would somehow become evil if they became free again. It would be more productive to wonder how we will avoid the evils toward which we are clearly headed if we don't become free again.

But rather than engage in either of these speculations, the more important question now is, *can* we become free again, practically speaking? This being America, let's assume we should if we could. But is there a realistic path to freedom from where we are now?

11. Freedom Now, Practically Speaking

Let's start by noting what won't work. All Republican candidates for president routinely talk about the need to get back to the Constitution. Some of them have offered a few proposals, such as eliminating some departments and agencies of government that would move us in that direction. And all of them have called for eliminating Obamacare, including Mitt Romney, who vows if elected to start the process of getting rid of it on his first day in office. As described above, proposals to eliminate departments invariably fall into the category of high-hanging fruit, pipe dreams with little or no realistic chance of passage even if the candidate that proposed them were to win election in a landslide, and no chance of getting back to the Constitution. Getting rid of Obamacare may be a similar non-starter.

Even without Obamacare, we will still face the full panoply of government run health care, including Medicare, Medicaid and all the government involvement in setting rates and practices where third parties pay the bill. The maze of government-regulated HMOs, insurance companies, hospitals, doctors, drug companies, subsidized research, etc. are run – and would still be run with or without Obamacare – under antitrust, patent and other laws, leaving little room for old-fashioned doctor-patient relationships, much less for the natural formation of health care networks that would otherwise form around the needs of patients and the capabilities of providers. In other words, we already had fully socialized medicine before Obamacare, and will have it afterwards under any proposals.

The universally reviled HMOs, for example, "are part of the solution, no matter which way you go," according to former Blackrock stock market strategist Bob Doll, meaning regardless of whether Obama or Romney wins in November. [cxxvi] As with the universally reviled high frequency trading in the stock market, antitrust and its perpetual multi-party competition cause the dysfunction in health care, too. HMOs are the point of contact for most people with health care services, and thus bear the brunt of public frustration. Natural networks cannot form under antitrust, and those that do form are broken up. So the public is always disappointed and angry – and mad at HMOs. Each political party attempts to tap into this anger at HMOs, and health care generally, to tout its own solutions.

The practical value to Republicans of harping on repeal of Obamacare is merely to identify themselves as red-blooded Red Team members who hate Obama and everything he stands for, especially all that Blue Team redistributionist socialism and nationalized health care. But as Newt Gingrich said in a moment of Republican candor, replacing Obama's left-wing social engineering with right-wing social engineering isn't a good idea either, [cxxvii] and it certainly isn't any closer to the Constitution.

Why are all the proposals unrealistic, with little or no chance to move us back toward the Constitution or away from socialism? The reason is that the proposals are not meant to be realistic. They are only meant to be provocative and antagonistic. The Red Team proposals are picked for their ability to rally the Red Team troops around an anti-Blue Team agenda. They are mirror images of similarly unrealistic Blue Team proposals seeking to rally Blue Team members around an anti-Red Team agenda. The proposals of both teams are attractive for their capacity to show as sharply as possible how minor differences in the socialist programs of both parties might matter, even if they really don't. But while Republicans would fiddle with vouchers or medical savings accounts or shopping for insurance across state lines, while Democrats would fiddle with individual mandates or a single payer system, the end result will be socialized medicine just as much under Romney or any other Republican president as under Obama or any other Democratic president.

Both the Red Team and the Blue Team are playing to their constituencies by highlighting the evils of the other side, by which both of them mean the flow of redistribution would be changed in the wrong direction if the other side wins in November. But in point of fact both teams would leave health care in the hands of government. And both teams score highest by fulminating about the evils that will ensue if the other team's experts are put in charge. Both teams talk about the urgent need to "save" Medicare, Medicaid, Social Security and the rest of the existing government array. That they have different ways of doing so, which favor their team's members over the other team's members, does not make either of them any less socialist, or get us any closer to the Constitution.

A shorthand way to think of the problem is to think about what would favor the rise of demagogues. That term is pejorative, of course. But if you spin it positively, what it really means is "leader" of the people against an oppressor. Just as Hitler, der Führer, led Germany against the oppressive terms of the Versailles Treaty, or Mussolini, Il Duce, led fascist Italy, or Karl Marx led workers against the oppression of capitalist bosses, demagogues' careers spring up when real or imagined oppression can be posited. The appeal is identical to the appeal of messiahs noted earlier, in which the hope is that the leader and his warriors can slay the other side's warriors and take their property.

What would favor the rise of demagogues? When property is in play, demagogues can sway almost anyone. So the trick to growing government is to put property in play. The current situation, in which every political issue can be presented as an oppressive injustice of distribution, is ideal for demagogues on both sides of the aisle. That being the case, it is not in the interest of any politician to try to move us, literally, back to the Constitution. That would restore property rights and thus cut off his potential to become a leader of his team, i.e., a demagogue. That is why everyone in both parties is happy to applaud "the Constitution," "freedom" and other patriotic symbols, but only as symbols. No one can seriously propose realistic means of getting back to the Constitution, because the Constitution would cut off his own and his teammates' potential to rise within their party. It is not in the interest of politicians to propose solutions that would actually work, because any time spent proposing them means forgoing time spent excoriating the other side, which is the real path to power.

What is good for demagogues, politically speaking, is the success of the opposition. The success of Red Team tax breaks for the rich is good for the Blue Team's demagogues. The success of the Blue Team at getting extended unemployment benefits is good for the Red Team's demagogues. All such successes create opportunities for demagogues on the opposing side, and these situations are self-feeding spirals. Republicans' success feeds Democrats' demagogues and Democrats' success feeds Republicans' demagogues.

Given these battles between demagogues, the last thing anyone who is serious about moving us back toward a true vision of liberty should do is get mixed up on that battlefield. Serious proposals would not do what the demagogues do, which is to pick battles for maximum heat and emotion, with little chance of or even desire for realistic political movement. Instead, serious proposals would seek issues that do not generate heat and emotion, but that if implemented, would make a real difference in liberty. What does this mean, practically speaking? It means that, while a plan to restore our right to the pursuit of happiness could head into the thicket of affirmative action, civil rights, union law, entitlements, taxes and other contentious fields where the Red and Blue divisions are lined up against each other, the better approach is to restore our rights first in areas where the stakes are not clear, where there are no divisions lined up, where some good could actually be done.

An attempt to eliminate the Department of Education, which administers Pell Grants and student loans, and distributes aid to public schools, and is beloved of teachers unions, all of which are downward redistribution sacred cows, would create maximum heat and have no chance of getting done. Furthermore, even if the Department of Education were eliminated, it is certain that most or all of its functions would be transferred elsewhere. Since the main problems in education are inherent to any system of public education, and since there is no plan to eliminate public education along with the Department of Education, the whole exercise would be a waste of time and political energy anyway.

Contrast this with an attempt to eliminate any antitrust agency. Here, the aforementioned confusion of theory and conflicts of application make for a much easier target. No one knows, including the experts, what good these agencies really do. The direction of redistribution is unclear. The Red and Blue teams are confused as to which side they favor on any particular dispute and usually wind up on the same side on the main issue of power for themselves and their cronies. Since lawyers, lobbyists, bureaucrats and other expert functionaries are not exactly sacred cows for anyone, and since what they do is at best unclear, and since it is by the main theory under which they operate not even supposed to have distribution consequences, there will be no protests in the streets, no banners and placards, no chanting hordes on any statehouse steps, if a proposal to eliminate these agencies is made.

Moreover, since every dot and comma of what they actually do is harmful to America, since there is no good whatsoever that comes from their existence, it would be much easier to contemplate their entire elimination. There would be no need to think about which departments to transfer their necessary functions to, because they don't have any necessary functions. Their entire purpose is to engage in witch-hunts to protect and aggrandize their own power. While other agencies are merely inefficient as they transfer wealth from one group to another, giving those groups great cause to protest any potential changes in the direction of redistribution, antitrust is a purely parasitic exercise in which the bureaucrats and experts serve only themselves. As far as the public is concerned, it is at best a mystery where the wealth is coming from and where it is going as a result of their murky machinations. With no easily identifiable winning or losing groups from the antitrust process, the likelihood of protests at the prospect of its elimination would be negligible. Losing these functions would be no greater loss than the loss of the witch-hunting Inquisition would have been to the Catholic Church.

Former SEC Chairman Arthur Levitt once said investors feel comforted just seeing the Chairman walk into the SEC's building in Washington. [cxxviii] The funny thing is, he wasn't kidding. If investors understood what the SEC has done, they certainly would not take comfort in it. The SEC's actions can be blamed for destroying the greatest market for capital raising and investing that ever existed and replacing it with a casino of rapid fire trading that investors loathe and that produces little capital. Millions of jobs have been lost or not created as a result. [cxxix] On the investor protection side, the SEC can be blamed for the creation of the Madoff business that then morphed under the SEC's not so watchful eyes into a Ponzi scheme. The National Market System and Madoff's business were, quite literally, made for each other [cxxx] under the deliberate plan by the SEC – in partnership with Madoff – to obliterate the dominant market shares of the NYSE and Nasdaq. [cxxxi] Among the results, in addition to obliterating those market shares and making Madoff rich before the Ponzi scheme and creating his reputation that enabled him to conduct the Ponzi scheme: the setting off of the collapse of the stock market in the late summer of 2007 that led to the credit crisis and the Great Recession; [cxxxii] the creation of high-frequency trading, which today only high-frequency traders love and everyone else is either bewildered by or hates; and the Flash Crash of May 6, 2010.

Many of these are unintended consequences, which are typically forgiven if the intentions of the agency causing them were well meaning and sincere. But this excuse has long since cloyed beyond its useful shelf life. As I said in *Countdown*, there will come a time when our forbearance for error should be withdrawn, since the piling up of so may errors is no longer forgivable when it becomes obvious that their proliferation alone invalidates the good intentions excuse. [cxxxiii] That time has come. While one can imagine fixing a glitch or two, fixing dozens or hundreds of them as they keep coming out of the woodwork is just not credible policy.

Moreover, we should not lose sight of the *intended* goal that underlies all of these errors and glitches, namely the extermination of the dominant market shares of the primary markets pursuant to the competition theories of antitrust. That goal has been accomplished in spades, so much so that the goal itself has become the subject of second-guessing by various committees in Congress and many experts. But any average citizen can easily see that going from a situation in which there was only one market for each stock, a condition that is implied in the very concept of a market as a centralizing and focusing facility, to a situation where there are over a dozen officially registered exchanges and many dozens of unregistered exchange-like apparitions, too, is the obvious reason we have high frequency trading, flash crashes and all the other black swan aberrations that keep cropping up. The fact that the SEC refuses to acknowledge any possibility that its policies may by the root cause of all of these problems is evidence of bad faith on the Commission's part. Such bad faith by itself is sufficient reason to get rid of the SEC.

Although these are all complex topics, it is clear if one delves into them that the SEC has done us no good and much harm. Except for lawyers, lobbyists, bureaucrats and politicians, no one would shed a tear at the Commission's passing, and even these would cry in private to avoid being associated with Wall Street or the SEC. The issues are too complex, theoretically confused and, like all antitrust issues, the direction of redistribution is unclear.

The elimination of antitrust agencies like the SEC would open the door again to the creation and further evolution of natural network monopolies like stock exchanges. It is a mystery that no one in Washington or in academia, for that matter, has noticed that stock exchanges originally came into existence only because their founders could pursue antitrust violations. In other words, the main stock exchanges in the world would not exist if antitrust had been around at their founding. The Commission's 78-year failure to do anything useful can be explained by the fact that it has been attempting the impossible, namely to make sense of the nonsensical notion that stock exchanges can exist under antitrust. So far, the Commission has only shown that it can destroy stock exchanges, a not surprising result when you realize that the basic purpose of antitrust is to destroy networks.

Getting rid of the SEC as part of getting rid of antitrust generally would not only allow stock exchanges to form again, it would allow for repair of the existing mess through natural competition. Contentious problems like high frequency trading and the dearth of IPOs would resolve themselves as networks are allowed to form again. Equally important, eliminating antitrust would enable the refurbishing and repair of other infrastructure elements in our society, too. And perhaps most importantly, since antitrust is blocking new industries from forming that may be even more valuable than the old ones, throwing off this wet blanket would allow Americans to again create millions of jobs and untold wealth for our society as creating the old industries did.

Our largest and most important industries have been squeezed and deformed under the thumb of antitrust, resulting in confused fragmentation where we need the consistent and unbroken connections of an entire network to provide good service. Ironically, the remedies of government almost always involve requiring by mandate some form of "universal service" to address "gaps" in coverage, when in fact the gaps exist primarily because antitrust has blocked the natural formation of the complete networks in the first place. Getting rid of antitrust could quickly address this problem. For example, in the absence of antitrust and the rest of government's socialized medicine that we have now with or without Obamacare, it is likely that health care would already have become a complete network monopoly that naturally served everyone, just as telephones would have, and air travel, and electric utilities, and postal service. Eliminating antitrust would allow such dysfunctional industries to repair themselves naturally.

Alleged remedies in the current environment have instead focused on the forced delivery of essential services as a "basic human right," such as all the versions of health care do. Also included in this "rights" expansion to fill gaps in dysfunctional industries are the public utilities customer bill of rights, the airline passenger bill of rights, the telephone customer bill of rights, the anti-bullying bill of rights and many others. There is a much easier way to eliminate the problems that are leading to all these ad hoc bills of rights: eliminate the agencies that are causing the problems.

Without antitrust, education infrastructures could form that might even make it possible to move past the Department of Education without the political bloodletting that a direct confrontation would involve. The reality is we have no idea how damaging the loss of our right to the pursuit of happiness has been to America, or how much more readily even the most intractable problems might solve themselves if it were restored.

Since we chose to shackle ourselves with socialism, we have been beset with one surprising malady after another, from Ponzi schemes, flash crashes, IPO debacles and trillion dollar deficits to the biggest surprise of all: 9/11. We simply cannot know, since we didn't go down that path, what freedom would have meant for these aberrations. Would they have occurred anyway, or would we have been spared? Since in any case they all did occur under the aegis of expanding socialism, we should beware of expanding government in response, lest we lurch even further into the destructive pathology that is causing the problems. The best bet for reversing the downward spiral is that we begin to restore the pursuit of happiness by ridding the land of antitrust. If we do, new industries we can't imagine now would be able to form as their predecessors did. New industries used to regularly renew our economy's ability to grow, and have created unbelievably large numbers of jobs. Without antitrust, they could do so again.

Americans once had the guts and the insight to revolt against tyranny. But that was when the source of it was an ocean away from us. Now we have become our own worst enemy, having created a tyranny at home that, to the untrained eye, has all the patriotic trappings of our Revolution. If we are fooled by this, if we no longer have the insight to recognize tyranny when it is staring us in the face, or the guts to call it what it is and root it out, then we may be destined to follow in the footsteps of the other tyrannies we fought against in the twentieth century, tyrannies that forced their own people on pain of death to follow their imperial policies in lockstep.

The signs are not positive. We still revere Abraham Lincoln, [cxxxiv] who was undoubtedly the most destructive demagogue we ever had as president. A white supremacist who wanted to deport *all* blacks back to Africa, slave *and* free, [cxxxv] an imperialist who destroyed the Constitution's restraint on central government, a warmonger whose unnecessary war killed 620,000 Americans, Lincoln is nonetheless remembered as our best or second best president, after Washington. His phrases still resonate, the ones that crafted a moral framework for the war based on emancipation, freedom, democracy, "with malice toward none, with charity for all" and all that. But what else could he do? It wouldn't have sounded right to have "loosed the fateful lightening of His terrible swift sword" just to collect the tariff, would it? [cxxxvi] A moral myth of freedom was needed to justify massive economic redistribution from the South to the North via the tariff, a myth that said the North was moral and the South was immoral based on attitudes toward slavery. [cxxxvii] But the myth is at best a post hoc justification for a conflict that arose in reality due to economic bullying. As chief demagogue and bully, Lincoln was able to reshape the story to suit his ends – and we bought it.

The evidence that the Civil War morality play had holes in it has been there all along. But we have chosen to not see them. We choose to remember instead the "with malice toward none, with charity for all" part of the second inaugural, rather than the Biblical invocation of a self-righteous revenge excuse for eviscerating the South that preceded it. Sounding every bit the vengeful messiah speaking for God, Himself, Lincoln gave the moral justification for killing hundreds of thousands of Southerners and taking their assets:

> Yet, if God wills that it continue until all the wealth piled up by the bondsman's two hundred and fifty years of unrequited toil shall be sunk, and until every drop of blood drawn with the lash shall be paid with another drawn with the sword, as was said three thousand years ago, so still it must be said "the judgments of the Lord are true and righteous altogether." [cxxxviii]

Seldom has such eloquence been applied in service of redistribution and violence by government to bring it about. Nor such a straightforward description of the vengeance motive underlying remedies such as reparations and affirmative action. After all the eloquence and scripture, however, we may again be attributing more to the man and less to the temper of the times than we should. Our enthusiastic acceptance of the moral myth of the Civil War may just be one more piece of evidence that Americans have chosen to be fooled by socialism because We-the-People wanted it and demanded it.

One person who was not fooled by the Lincoln whitewash was Adolf Hitler, who admired Lincoln as he admired Bismarck for consolidating imperial power. [cxxxix] And Lincoln himself was quite clear that his "paramount object" was not to free slaves but to "save the Union."

> If I could save the Union without freeing *any* slave I would do it, and if I could save it by freeing *all* the slaves I would do it; and if I could save it by freeing some and leaving others alone, I would also do that. What I do about slavery, and the colored race, I do because I believe it helps to save the Union; and what I forbear, I forbear because I do *not* believe it would help to save the Union. [cxl]

The true legacy of the Civil War is not the moral myth of freedom, but the imperial reality of American power. If we Americans cannot be half as perceptive as Hitler was about Lincoln, then the most likely outcome is that we will breed our own Hitler out of the demagogic opportunities bubbling up from our own redistribution conflicts. If we are able to avoid this fate, it will be due to the insight of our Founders, who left us a very practical instruction. They knew that mere men could not know everything and, therefore, that it would be unwise to let government design our world for us. All we have to know is that protecting our right to the pursuit of happiness is the right thing to do.

12 Legacy

Some are fond of saying these days, "the United States is not Greece." Greece of course is the poster child for how caving to excessive public workers' wage and benefit demands, which are effectively redistributions from taxpayers, can lead to out-of-control debt, and ultimately to violent protests in the streets when a country has to pull back from commitments it can't afford. Greece is also the poster child for how the inevitable bankruptcy, bailouts and contagion that follow such profligacy can occupy all the world's major powers, even though Greece is only a tiny blip on world economic growth or decline, as the case may be. It's true the United States is not Greece. But the comparison is not a favorable one.

Greece does not have the capital of the United States nor the ability therefore to rescue itself. But America today is suffering from a far worse case of the Greek disease than Greece is. The grip of public employee entitlements is at least as unyielding and politically irreversible as it is in Greece, and has already resulted in clashes in the streets, or on the statehouse steps in Wisconsin, for example. But unlike Greece, the public employee entitlement problem is only the tip of the iceberg in America. The problem here extends throughout the entire industrial infrastructure, not just public service jobs. And the entitled beneficiaries include the entire ruling elite of America, the whole class of legal experts and their business and political cronies who design and run our world. Greece is lucky: a few protests, a decade of depression, and they're done. The end of America's similar problem is likely to be far worse, and may include the end of America.

The economic strength of America, while massive, is unwinding quickly. Largely a legacy of the infrastructure built by the Robber Barons, we have been coasting on their capital for over a century now, even as we progressively dismantle the political commitment to freedom that enabled it. In recent years we have been beset by multiple crises in all the industries the Robber Barons created – oil, railroads, steel, electric utilities, telecom, automobiles, airlines – which are now just rubble-strewn battlefields where fights over redistribution occur.

But the best example of this pattern is the most important industry of capitalism, the stock market where capital is raised, and the problems there are accelerating quickly. With regulators now responding to the high-frequency monsters they created, such as the Flash Crash, the IPO debacles, and the Knightmare of August 1, 2012, with massive increases in their power and more rules of exactly the type that caused these problems, it is clear that America's days as the leading creator of new industries are over. We killed the Goose – the New York Stock Exchange and Nasdaq – and smashed her Golden Eggs, such as Standard Oil and Wintel. We have now replaced them all with government bureaucracies that are universally failing, none more so than in the capital markets industry. Not only are ongoing antitrust efforts destroying the successful companies that emerged from the creation process, the creation process itself is dying because of the SEC's power-grab.

When the BATS IPO failed, and then, much more spectacularly, Facebook's IPO failed too, both in embarrassing debacles for their exchanges, high frequency trading was blamed, as usual. But this understates the problem. High frequency was at fault, but only indirectly this time. The real culprit was the SEC's hidden hand behind the structure of fixed time single price call auctions, or "calls," such as are used for opens and closes, and for IPOs and circuit breakers. These key facilities have been distorted under Commission guidance to make way as much as possible for continuous high frequency trading. Deliberately or accidentally, continuous high frequency trading has become the physical embodiment of the Commission's four-decade crusade to create an electronic National Market System, and the Commission has a strong interest in protecting its baby. Preventing efficient calls from emerging is now the main practical means by which the Commission shelters and coddles its high frequency creation, and thereby preserves its own role in designing and overseeing markets.

In the early years of this century, the SEC forced the markets to adopt electronic calls at the open and close of trading largely through behind the scenes arm-twisting that was not visible to the public. All regulated markets are familiar with how this works. Since they all need Commission cooperation on rule filings and other issues, if the Commission wants something, it is imprudent to resist. Cooperating with what the Commission wants becomes the quid pro quo that obtains Commission cooperation on what an exchange wants. Sometime around 2001, the Commission decided on its own and without public notice and comment that markets that wanted to become or remain registered exchanges had to open and close with electronic single price call auctions. The SEC designed its call market model secretly in Washington and then strong-armed the markets to accept it by insisting behind the scenes on certain rules. [cxli] With minor modifications, the SEC's model is still the one used for the electronic opening and closing mechanisms the NYSE and Nasdaq use today. Unfortunately, the Commission's meddling has resulted in a hodgepodge of mingled purpose rules for both continuous markets and call markets that messes both of them up and leads exchanges into errors like the Facebook IPO structure, which could hardly have been more poorly or naïvely designed.

It is not that the SEC designed the Facebook IPO structure that Nasdaq used, but that the starting point for Nasdaq's design undoubtedly assumed SEC approval would be easier if its auctions for IPOs were based as much as possible on the kind of calls the Commission has insisted on for opens and closes. But as auctions these opening and closing calls are themselves very poorly designed, primarily because they are hopelessly entangled in continuous market processes and priorities in order to foster high frequency trading. That Nasdaq could describe the Facebook IPO problem as beginning when the "auction" took 5 milliseconds instead of the expected 3 milliseconds is a sign of how inappropriately the mechanisms the markets have adopted at SEC insistence are structured. [cxlii]

And that Nasdaq actually believed it needed to allow cancellations and new orders to be accommodated during the 5 millisecond period when the auction program was running – as if it too were a continuous high frequency trading process – shows how bamboozled by the SEC's model the exchange was. Both the Nasdaq IPO model, and before it the BATS IPO model, were reportedly tested extensively. But both failed miserably either because they were inappropriately trying to mimic continuous trading processes (Nasdaq), or couldn't manage the switchover to continuous trading after the allegedly "successful" auction (BATS). [cxliii]

Glitches and bugs can be fixed, at least in theory. But the ones that allegedly caused these IPO debacles cannot be fixed, because they are not just bugs. They are all direct or indirect consequences of NMS policies designed to promote continuous high frequency trading. It is precisely because the SEC and the industry are so fixated on continuous trading that the aberrations are occurring. They are happening because regulators have blocked effective calls not designed by them, such as those that were run by human beings at the NYSE, or the electronic AZX auction, which was blocked by, among other things, requiring it to operate off hours.

A good call market runs on an entirely different set of rules and principles than does continuous trading. Call markets and continuous trading can coexist relatively easily, but only if continuous trading runs outside the calls without disturbing them. Both are price discovery mechanisms that must operate on their own. Just as it would be impossible to imagine simultaneous auctions of the same painting in two different auction houses, it is not possible to have both the continuous market and the call market operate alongside each other while taking account of each other's orders and rules at the same time. It is a nonstarter to imagine that calls can somehow run in the midst of continuous trading rules, such as the Reg. NMS trade-through rule that connects all the continuous high frequency markets. This nonstarter is precisely what the SEC is pretending to engineer, as if the continuous market and the call market were going to a dance together. It can only have the effect of preventing calls from succeeding.

Why is the SEC so anxious to protect continuous trading? Why is it so anxious to avoid effective calls? The answer is simple: its power and its survival depend on these policies.

Continuous trading lends itself well to antitrust-based deregulation, the SEC's natural habitat and the source of all its power. Call markets, in contrast, because they are *not* continuous, actually *can* solve the problems of continuous high frequency trading, such as flash crashes, IPO debacles, Knightmares and other "software glitches." But the SEC's natural habitat of continuous trading cannot include effective calls or the habitat will disintegrate. In fact, effective calls would be so good at cleaning up the debacles and black swans of continuous trading that they could spell the end of the SEC's involvement in market structure.

The power of calls derives largely from the fact that they are natural monopolies in a way that continuous trading is not. To grasp why this is so, think about how impossible it would be for two call markets in the same stock to continue for long in competition with each other. As network scientists know, the market would soon tip toward a winner and the loser would die. This is most obvious when contemplating two call markets operating at the same time. But it would also be true of call markets competing at different times, because the action would still gravitate to the more successful call and eventually tip in its direction, leaving the loser to retire from the field.

Such tipping and winner-take-all situations as we would see for call market competition *if it were allowed to occur* are decidedly not characteristic of today's continuous electronic trading competition, which can support virtually infinite numbers of clones competing with each other. This was not always true. In fact, the opposite was true in the times before the SEC forced the markets to become electronic via NMS. NMS is a typical antitrust-based "deregulation" that forces competition on incumbent monopolies, in this case by requiring them to open their markets up to many free-riding competitors by making the incumbents' orders transparent and immediately electronically executable. The Order Handling rules adopted in 1997 had this effect on the Nasdaq universe of stocks, and the Reg. NMS trade-through rule adopted in 2007 had this effect on the NYSE universe.

But before such antitrust-based reforms squeezed out anticompetitive practices and loyalty oaths that bound members to their exchanges, such as former NYSE Rule 390, there were many social-inclusion and social-exclusion features of human trading that created powerful tipping points and winner-take-all situations in traditional exchange formation. It was these features and forces that led naturally to all of the dominant incumbent monopoly markets in the world today that are now in the process of being busted. Deregulation under NMS brought an end to those methods as the SEC, with occasional assists by the Justice Department's Antitrust Division, busted the NYSE and Nasdaq. The continuous electronic markets that have replaced manual trading are now easily deregulated away from tipping points to maintain perpetual multi-party competition with no winners – hence, the clones. This is why in the SEC's natural habitat of deregulation, markets must not only remain electronic, but they must remain continuous. In short the Commission created a perpetually expanding mission for itself by busting the markets on antitrust grounds and mandating continuous high frequency trading in the National Market System. Call market formation, in contrast, depends only on natural preferential attachment – liquidity begets liquidity – and thus presents no antitrust violations to bust. If call markets took hold, the SEC would be left with no one to bust and nothing to do.

But the uncomfortable problem for the SEC is that, by its own admission (not to mention obvious reality), all of the solutions to today's market structure problems involve somehow utilizing the power of calls to do things only calls can do, such as to settle things down, to find consensus prices, to provide a "time out," a "pause" or a "circuit breaker" from the chaos of continuous trading. However obvious and promising such answers might be, the SEC will undoubtedly continue to block them or make sure they don't work. Just as AZX was blocked, and just as the NYSE's and Nasdaq's opening processes were blocked when the SEC forced them to accept its poorly designed opening and closing calls, the Commission will continue to block all effective calls, because it will glimpse its own demise in their success. The latest plan to install a limit-up/limit-down regime as a circuit breaker, for example, is clearly designed to preserve continuous trading as much as possible. At best, these confusing limit-up/limit-down restraints will fall back on the haphazard hybrids of continuous and call market trading the exchanges use at opens and closes, which are ill suited to markets under stress, as they would be by definition in limit-up/limit-down situations.

Once a call gets a toehold, it would be highly likely to spread as network effects take over and a new stock market network would form. Due to the natural preferential attachment of liquidity-begets-liquidity, it would do so without resort to any anticompetitive practices. It would just happen. There would be no need for conspiracies, cartels, price fixing, tying, market division or any other forms of deliberate monopolizing. Calls would grow naturally into dominant monopolies without having to resort to any of the social inclusion or social exclusion methods that enabled the old exchanges to become dominant. A good call for an IPO would soon be used as a circuit breaker. A good circuit breaker would be used to open the market. A good opening call would be used to close the market.

I do not make these points as prelude to a claim that calls are superior to continuous markets because they don't need antitrust violations to succeed. By now my support for the old markets' methods as expressions of their legitimate rights under natural law should be clear. But as a matter of regulatory politics, it is necessary at this point to appreciate the mortal threat that calls present to the SEC. Even if several markets started out competing to be the opening call in a stock, and even if their calls were identically structured, the market would tip to one of them, and stay there at least for a while due to lock-in. At some point, only one market would be where all the call market action occurred in every stock. That wouldn't have to be the same market for all stocks, although it could be. But it could also be that all of the NYSE stocks traded only in the NYSE's calls and not Nasdaq's or anyone else's calls, and all of the Nasdaq stocks traded only in Nasdaq's calls and not NYSE's or anyone else's.

But it could also be that the winner of the competition for calls would be a single market. NYSE, for example, could wind up doing the calls in all of its listed stocks *and* all of Nasdaq's listed stocks, too. Or Nasdaq or BATS or Direct Edge could wind up with all of the calls in all stocks, regardless of where they were listed. It could also be that a non-registered ECN, ATS or even a dark pool or a foreign market, could wind up in control of all the calls.

No one knows what share of total volume would go to calls versus continuous trading. My own guess is that it would be well north of 30%. But it could be 60% or 90%. And what if just one market, say, the NYSE, did all the calls in all stocks and, because of that, seemed to get more than its share of the continuous trading between the calls, too? It would not make much sense under those circumstances to go through all the rigmarole and expense of co-locating at umpteen markets to play the fragmented high frequency game anymore, would it? Since a properly structured call market is a slow moving, deliberate and calm event, there might be little need for co-locating at all anymore. Most traders would find it perfectly efficient to just stick with the NYSE for both call market trading and continuous trading, and would skip co-location. Obviously the SEC and its high frequency supporters would not be happy with those outcomes. If enough traders dropped co-location, then most or all of the clones would disappear and the high frequency dragon would die a natural death, ending the SEC's raison d'être.

Every one of these scenarios would be directly contradictory to every policy and goal of the SEC for the last four decades. But every one of them would bring about a better market than the one the SEC has given us. The SEC will, therefore, continue to do everything it can to prevent any of these efficient outcomes from occurring. It will continue to block well structured calls from being used. It will continue to insist that its own improperly designed calls be used at opens and closes. And it will continue to stand idly by when, under its guidance, markets make inane use of off-the-shelf features of these poorly designed calls to do their IPOs.

The obvious problem in the Facebook IPO was ideological reliance on continuous trading, which prevented running an effective call. This result in turn was foreordained by the Commission's NMS and its predilection toward continuous high frequency trading. Nasdaq can analyze the failure from a technology perspective all it wants as it looks for its "bug." But the answer will certainly be that its Facebook IPO was inappropriately letting last-millisecond orders and cancellations pollute the efficient running of the call, an obvious answer that it takes no technology expertise to recognize. The real question is: Why was Nasdaq so foolishly fixated on continuous trading? And the answer to that is that the SEC's National Market System demands it. The National Market System is the reigning regulatory regime under which the SEC is doing everything in its power to make sure the thriving U.S. capital market it killed stays dead so the Commission can continue to thrive by installing its replacement.

Greece never had such a great market, and so didn't have it to lose. But the loss of this advantage for America will be devastating to its citizens' expectations. We have come to rely on our country's ability to create grand advances for our civilization, including whole new categories of activity and industries, as if they sprang from some exceptional spirit or character, as opposed to the freedom we had. The problem is that we now feel entitled to the greatness, but the freedom that created it is gone. Our comedown, therefore, will be gut wrenching, as the relative paucity of our present potential compared to our past will take away our hope. Greece won't have to suffer that grand comedown. Greece can simply go bankrupt and go on, its demagogues only footnotes in history, little remembered even in Greece and forgotten everywhere else. The United States may suffer a much worse fate.

The thing about demagogues is they can come out of nowhere and quickly dominate the board. Politically speaking, they can "go viral" in the blink of an eye. Once mobs have been coached by politically correct dishonesty into ignoring violations of natural law, almost any incendiary issue can ignite the big one. We are bemused and bewildered that "American culture may be on its way to phasing out the gendered roles of 'husband and wife' and 'father and mother' and replacing them with the functional roles of 'spouse and parent'." [cxliv] But the countries we are extending our model to through force are confused at best, and more likely angry, as the angriest ones dream of Shariah, jihad and attacking New York. Such conditions are perfect for the rise of demagogues and final solutions that would eclipse the Holocaust in horror. Such a legacy would also eclipse the memory of America as the shining city on a hill, a beacon of freedom where the laws of nature and of nature's God were honored.

Americans cannot imagine such an end, of course. Yet if we look around, if we gaze across the totality of our society at all of its challenges, it becomes harder and harder to ignore the possibility, indeed the likelihood, that we are headed for just such a conclusion. That it took the utter collapse of our State Department's effort to build an Iraqi police force before we decided to shrink back from it with our tail between our legs and $8 billion down the drain [cxlv] is but one of many examples of our never-ending attempts at final solutions. None of them individually look like final solutions at first, but they are all part of the interconnected lattice of government solutions to everything that have come to characterize America today. When it comes to finding solutions to all of our problems caused by government, more government is always the solution offered by government.

Never Again is the usual slogan for *all* solutions. Whether to the original Holocaust, or to the panoply of problems the Dodd Frank rules are supposed to prevent, or to the glitches and bugs in our stock market, we seem addicted under Never Again to doing more of whatever interventions we were applying when the problems arose. So why wouldn't we expect that in those most dangerous areas, where death and drones, where killing people we don't know the names of, [cxlvi] where loosing weapons of mass destruction and losing cities are possible – why wouldn't we at least worry that an awful legacy is in store?

When empires are on the march bent on extending their redistribution ideals, the end is never good; in fact it is always horrific. Whether their crusades and "just wars" are launched in the name of slaves, Aryans, or the proletariat, the record is clear: millions will die and the alleged beneficiaries will not actually benefit. [cxlvii] After the collapse, there is only the memory of death camps, gulags and senseless slaughters. Changing the names and slogans isn't likely to change the pattern, either. However sure we are of the beneficence of our own crusades on behalf of egalitarian democratic pluralism to aid the world's oppressed, poor, hungry, women, minorities, etc., which are the global mirror images of our domestic redistribution crusades on behalf of similarly aggrieved groups – women, minorities, the middle class, the 99% – we are fooling ourselves if we think changing the names and slogans will change the pattern. Hope and optimism for a better result this time are just our way of whistling past the graveyard of history.

There was a time when electronic trading in a National Market System was a final solution of sorts. NMS believers thought it would solve all problems in our markets. The need for market making or any other form of intermediation would disappear as buyers met sellers directly on the transparent screens. It would be the ultimate in fairness, a level playing field where the lowliest retail investor got the same treatment as the richest insiders.

Several decades into that dream, it is clear if nothing else that we did not get it right the first time. But each new iteration, reform, order-handling rule, Reg. NMS or bug fix is still touted as the final answer. Even though trading costs are now negligible fractions of their pre-NMS levels, the latest proposed solution for this non-problem is to cut the tick size even further, to one tenth of the current penny, in order to remove the allegedly illegitimate "distortion" that professional market making is still taking out of the market. [cxlviii] And even though the largest market maker to retail embarrassingly wiped out more than all of its capital and masses of retail confidence in forty minutes of market-making mayhem in the Knightmare of August 1, 2012, SEC Chairman Mary Schapiro can only brag about how well the Commission's circuit breakers worked to contain the damage, promising the Commission is looking to find even better solutions to improve confidence in the future. [cxlix]

One wonders if investor confidence can fall below zero, as Knight Capital's capital did. While contemplating that, it is worth reminding ourselves that Knight is the largest and latest dominant example of the electronic market making model the SEC and Bernie Madoff worked together to fashion as the final solution to intermediation costs in their National Market System. They did not expect this utopian dream would lead to high frequency trading instead. But it did. And the great irony and danger is that the Commission cannot and will not admit that it is therefore the author of all of the debacles that are occurring today, and that high frequency trading is enabling them all. The reason the SEC cannot admit this is that its own fate is inextricably tied to high frequency trading.

This stock market scenario is playing out throughout Western societies in all areas of human endeavor. Everywhere we are engaged in endless strings of interventions to exterminate natural networks and replace them with government designs that will finally level the playing field. Just as the SEC took a stock market structure that was working wonders before the Commission got involved, and has been wreaking havoc with its "new and improved" designs ever since, every major industry is subject to similar reshaping maneuvers by government agencies. And although we are a long way down this eugenic path in every industry and are consequently experiencing problems everywhere – and thus should know better – we continue to make matters worse. To every malfunction and dysfunction, we are adopting more of the same reform policies that were being newly followed when the pathologies first emerged and, by all logical and honest analysis, are at least prime candidates for being their causes. Yet the one remedy we never consider in any situation, not even as a last resort, is the one America's Founders said should be our first, last and only choice, namely freedom. Instead, we continue to subvert the laws of nature and of nature's God with government solutions that are digging us deeper into the same hole.

That we cannot recognize the patent office's first-to-file Hail Mary or the SEC's circuit breakers as final solutions that won't work are but a few of hundreds of examples of the pervasive dishonesty that is blinding us to the right answers. It is dishonest to pin our hopes for capital formation on the JOBS Act, or even on demanding that the SEC require call auctions for IPOs. [cl] As promising as these solutions may sound, their authors misunderstand the failures that occasioned their introduction. It's not that we didn't get the structure right, although we didn't. It's that we insisted on designing the structure ourselves, instead of letting it form naturally. The lesson we should be learning is that eugenics doesn't work. Instead we are just jumping from one eugenic solution to another. A society that can make such mistakes as the general rule rather than the exception is a society that is headed very fast in the wrong direction. It is in fact a society that is desperately seeking a final, final solution.

13. When Truth is Treason

Around the time of the American Revolution, there was a debate between those who saw our separation from England as the founding of a new unified nation, and those who saw it as a separation by each of the individual colonies from England, united only to help each other accomplish the separation. With the Redcoats primarily on their minds, this may have seemed like a distinction without a difference. But the difference was real, has never been settled, and has precipitated the greatest conflicts in our history, from the Civil War to today's disputes over health care and the War on Terror. The single nation or Federalist side was associated with Alexander Hamilton, and the separate independent states side was associated with Thomas Jefferson.

The Jeffersonian Democrats, as they have come to be called, were concerned with the potential for their new federation to take on the despotic powers of the tyranny they left behind. To forestall that eventuality, the Tenth Amendment in the Bill of Rights and other measures and statements were adopted to allow states to decline to follow laws the central government might unjustly impose on them. The means by which states would do this included nullification and secession. This view saw the Revolution itself as essentially a secession of the American colonies from the British Empire and their establishment as independent sovereign states or countries. Without the Bill of Rights giving them power to resist any tyranny imposed by the new federal government, ratification of the Constitution might not have happened, in spite of the fact that, as James Madison said when he introduced the Tenth Amendment, the powers listed in it were already in the Constitution without it. It was a sort of constitutional belt-and-suspenders approach to making sure we stayed free. The approach apparently worked to secure ratification; staying free was another matter.

Madison was an ally recruited by Hamilton to help write The Federalist papers under Roman pseudonyms, which were basically essays in favor of ratifying the Constitution. The Hamiltonian Federalists didn't see the Revolution the way the Jeffersonian Democrats did. They saw the new unified United States as a nation in its own right that would assume powers as such. The rights, liberties, privileges and immunities guaranteed in the Constitution would be up to the national government to define, provide and protect. States would have representation in that national government, but could not nullify its laws or secede from it.

By the early nineteenth century a variety of major issues mostly involving tariffs caused nullification to be used and secession to be threatened. Southern states saw excessively high tariffs as harmful to them economically, and observed that revenues from them went to finance railroads and other infrastructure in the northern states. They saw the tariff as essentially a massive scheme of redistribution from the South to the North, sucking economic vitality out of the South and pushing the North into a boom ignited by government spending. Illinois railroad lawyer and lobbyist Abraham Lincoln rode these issues to the top of the new Republican Party promising to not let the secessionists get away with nullifying tariffs again, as South Carolina did in the 1830s, which almost led to secession and civil war then. With the hardening of positions as Lincoln assumed the presidency, these issues did lead to the Civil War when, in quick succession, South Carolina and other southern states seceded, the Confederacy was formed and fired on Fort Sumter to force Union troops to leave it, and Lincoln – as promised in his first inaugural address – took military action to force collection of the tariff when on April 19, 1861 he blockaded southern ports. [cli]

Jeffersonian Democrats and Hamiltonian Federalists agree that the Civil War destroyed any rights of nullification or secession that may or may not have been in the Constitution. Jeffersonian descendents today nonetheless argue feebly that "states' rights" and the words in the key amendments must still be taken into consideration when the Supreme Court rules on issues like President Obama's health care plan or on budget matters or foreign wars. And a variety of libertarian think tanks and Red Team TV personalities and Republicans in Congress or seeking the presidency argue ad nauseam that we have to get back to the Constitution, as if intoning a few old ignored words would do the trick. It won't.

Moreover, since the debate between the Hamiltonian Federalists and the Jeffersonian Democrats was never settled, and both camps can still cite elements of their views in the written words of the Constitution and other histories, getting back to the Constitution wouldn't necessarily mean anything anyway. The reality is that getting back to the Constitution is a lost cause. Having already proved that we can go with the socialist flow, regardless of the words, the laws, the fine phrases about "limited government" and "enumerated powers," the "powers not delegated to the United States" being "reserved to the states respectively, or to the people," it is senseless to pretend the Constitution can save us now, when all it has proved so far is that – in spite of the Founders' heroic efforts – the Constitution has abandoned us. Or we have abandoned it; it's hard to tell the difference. Few better examples of the uselessness of Constitutional restraint exist than the many undeclared wars that have been launched and waged without the required declaration of war by Congress. From Lincoln's blockade of southern ports to the Vietnam War to the many fronts in the War on Terror, it is clear that presidents can violate the Constitution virtually at will. No wonder the right to the pursuit of happiness has also disappeared.

The only hope now is that we might be able to take some practical steps to reboot America in the spirit of the Declaration of Independence, which was a much clearer formulation of American ideals and, for all its brevity, a better script to follow for their practical implementation. We need not abandon or repeal any parts of the Constitution to do this, although ultimately we may want to strike the Copyright Clause in which patent authority resides. (Alternatively, we could simply ignore it, as we have so much of the rest of the Constitution.) But if our laws were not so long ago interpretable as not requiring antitrust, they could be again interpretable in that fashion. Doing so could start the unwinding of the long and destructive diversion we have taken away from our right to the pursuit of happiness. And because restoring that right domestically would also demonstrate the value of freedom of association more generally, it could also point the way out of the wars and "entangling alliances" [clii] we have blundered into abroad.

We will need to understand where we went wrong so we can restart the engine of freedom. Here again network science may help, this time by giving us perspective to think through the issues in the old Jefferson versus Hamilton debate, but in a new way. Forming alliances or dissolving bonds is the business of preferential attachment. It is necessary for the efficient formation of networks to allow nodes to freely form or disappear, to make links or decline to make links with other nodes, and to dissolve links when no longer preferred. Similarly, the efficient formation of states, countries and government networks will occur if alliances are free to form or dissolve pursuant to the legal commitments made in treaties, constitutions and similar documents establishing them. In other words, networks do their thing in a thoroughly Jeffersonian manner. Nullification and secession are as common to networks as any other laws of nature would be.

The Hamiltonian side of the argument pushes in the opposite direction. Preferential attachment is often overridden at critical junctures, as government grows by dictating whether to make or not make associations, alliances or connections. Preferred attachments are disallowed or broken, and sometimes even abhorrent ones are mandated – e.g., those "entangling alliances." While the choice of attachment may be styled as a preferred one, or at least one that is correct, efficient or good for one reason or another, the opportunity to be part of the power elite that makes the choice is all that really matters to anyone near the seat of power, and becomes the dominating dynamic of growth. Competition for that privilege causes factions to form, like the Red Team and the Blue Team, and demagogues to rise to lead them by vilifying the other side as evil incarnate.

Such factions invariably further their causes through coercion rather than freedom. They send the Army or the National Guard to emancipate slaves or enforce desegregation, or send soldiers and drones to require pluralist democracy. Whatever one thinks about the wisdom of such policies, the point here is that the enforcement mechanism is inconsistent with the preferential attachment of natural network formation, which must be voluntary or it will not work. Under preferential attachment, states would be allowed to secede if they want to. And secession could go the other way, too. If the federal government does not agree with a given state's policies or laws, and the people of the national government authorize it to do so, it is the federal government itself that could "secede" from the state by expelling it from the Union. All association or disassociation among and between states and nations would be voluntary. The tools of force and war would be deployed only for policing or self-defense, never to require attachments that are not preferred or are no longer preferred.

While the conflict between factions drives the growth of government, curiously, one of the original arguments for a large federal government was its presumed better ability to counteract such factions. As argued by James Madison in Federalist #10 and Federalist #51, the risk that property would be taken away by majorities was claimed to be greater in smaller polities, like states, than in larger ones, like the combination of all the states in the United States. This was one of the arguments in favor of ratifying the new Constitution that played well with those who were reluctant to ratify. These people feared that arbitrary and tyrannical takings of property might arise without a variety of checks and balances in place.

Favored methods of imposing restraint included the separation of powers among the different branches of government recommended by Montesquieu, [cliii] the Fifth Amendment in the Bill of Rights, which outlawed takings of private property for public use without just compensation and, if all else failed, the aforementioned autonomous rights of individual states to nullify unjust laws or secede from the United States. It is curious that Madison, one of Hamilton's Federalist allies, posed the size of the whole country as one of the protections against tyranny in this argument, which sounded at least similar to the other arguments against a large and powerful federal government. But in this case Madison turned those other arguments upside down, claiming that size and the power that would come with it would actually be restraining forces in themselves, at least compared to the necessarily smaller states.

I don't think Madison was disingenuous or jesting. But in retrospect, it certainly could appear so. In any case, we now have a very large and powerful federal government, which in contrast to Madison's expectations has managed to throw off all restraint as it redistributes property among the factions Madison feared, which bully their way into temporary majorities just as he worried they would in smaller polities. Strangely, as our government increasingly assumes these dictatorial powers, both domestically and internationally, these two Federalist papers, #s 10 and 51, have become the most revered of the lot, a total of eighty-five of them.

The popularity of these two essays, combined with the clear failure of their central claim that big government would restrain factions, should give us pause. The fact is that every single one of the hoped for restraints on government, from Madison's large government, to separation of powers, to states' rights, to the Constitution generally, the Bill of Rights, the Tenth Amendment, the Fifth Amendment, etc., all of them – singly and in combination – have proved somewhere between useless and counterproductive at restraining the growth of government. Taken together with the still fulsome belief in "the American system of government," whatever that means, as partly evidenced by the popularity of Federalist #10 and Federalist #51, our continuing confidence in evidently failed policies tells a cautionary tale, one which should be worrying us, but isn't. Being wrong, it seems, is no barrier to being certain. Stated another way, the more we fail, the more confident we seem to become that we are right. In terms of our sincere desire to get back to the principles of liberty America was founded on, the most important thing to realize at this point is that our original plan for preserving freedom failed. Our heart was in the right place. And freedom worked wonders while it lasted. But what we did to preserve it didn't work.

Obviously some humility is in order. The fact that it is nowhere to be found is both preventing solutions at home and sinking us ever deeper into a reflexive belligerence abroad that has itself become the chief danger to our economic and physical security. No longer viewed as a benign force, a live and let live exemplar that recognizes and respects the value of liberty to all men, we now have a particular view, an interest, and an ax to grind. Pushing pluralism, redistribution and democracy, we are increasingly coming up against peoples that for whatever reason resist our example. And we increasingly demand, at the point of guns and drones, that it's our way or the highway. We should have known it would come to this. A country that can persistently vilify John D. Rockefeller and glorify Abraham Lincoln must have a screw loose somewhere. But so sure of ourselves were we that we never noticed when "freedom" coming from us began to sound like tyranny to others.

Time is not on our side. Nor are the numbers. When General Grant at President Lincoln's behest pursued "total war," throwing Union soldiers into suicidal battles with Confederate soldiers, fully expecting that tens of thousands of his own men would be killed, he did so knowing this strategy would ultimately win the war, since the North had a larger population than the South, and could always conscript more. The strategy worked. The war was far more devastating proportionally to the South, killing or maiming for life three quarters of its men of military age. [cliv]

Now the tables are turned. However brave and skilled our soldiers are, the expense of supporting them to and through the conversion of everyone else to pluralistic democracy is a mission impossible. In contrast, the enemy we can barely name for fear of profiling, and would not be an enemy but for our own belligerent demand that it adopt our new version of democracy, has an endless supply of suicide soldiers looking for our weak spots. Muslim societies have a birth rate that is significantly greater than that in Western societies, and have shown an increasing capacity to inspire a radical few to hide and multiply in virtually every country, including our own, and to fling themselves at us in suicide missions. Consequently, the longer this conflict goes on, the more likely it is that we will lose a city. When that or something similarly surprising and devastating happens, it is certain that the War on Terror will ratchet up dramatically.

Politicians pin our hopes on winning Muslim hearts and minds through democracy to suppress this risk, as if the tiny minority of truly radical ones willing to attack us were controllable through elections. We should know better. Given that since the Progressive Era we ourselves have been seesawing between upward and downward redistribution every decade or two, it has been clear that even our own showcase of democracy is no longer able to find consensus through elections, and that there are always at least very large minorities that wish the last election had gone the other way. How much more impossible is it to imagine, then, such a successful hearts-and-minds campaign that it would dry up not just a majority, but *all* of the support for radicalization in the Muslim world? And it would need to be that successful in order to accomplish our goals. Unless *all* Muslims turned against supporting attacks on America, such attacks are bound to find sufficient support to continue. If they do, the us-against-them war of civilizations engendered by the War on Terror is not likely to diminish, ever. In fact, it is almost certain to continue generating more enemies than friends of America, and an ever-increasing likelihood of devastating attacks on America.

Essential to the struggle on both sides is the primal need to identify friends and enemies. During World War I, we adopted a law that made it illegal, treasonous actually, to say bad things about American policy, American soldiers, the look of their uniforms, or anything else that might be construed as non-supportive of the war effort. [clv] We sent hundreds of people to prison for years merely for saying certain words. It may seem as if the War on Terror has a long way to go to get that paranoid. But it doesn't, because it is supplemented by political correctness, under which Americans already hide their feelings, views and thoughts. This lack of candor, this dishonesty, is the true threat to America. If we have lost the ability to acknowledge or discuss openly the dangers we face, it is hard to see how we will avoid them.

There is at least a virtual conspiracy of silence in some quarters. In expert-driven agencies like the SEC, it is as if the agency itself were alive, with an ambition to protect and extend its own power as far as possible. All the people working at the agency and at all of the firms regulated by it and all of those working in the fields affected by it instinctively learn how to shape their thoughts and demeanor and personal ambitions to conform to the agency's ambition. Those who fail to learn and conform are shunned.

For example, when reporting on recent debacles, members of the press are wise to refer to them as "glitches" or "bugs," implying first that they really aren't such a big deal and can be easily corrected by reprogramming, second that they might have been caused by insufficient compliance with SEC rules on software development and testing, and third that future bugs can be prevented, either by better compliance or more rules. Reporters chime in on the SEC's preferred narrative that problems like these are due to the SEC not having had the tools to keep up with the fast-moving industry in the high frequency age. This narrative implies that more resources, surveillance and enforcement are necessary, thus buttressing the Commission's requests for more funds from Congress to buy more computers, hire more lawyers and software engineers, and generally bulk up the agency so glitches will never again happen.

Most implausibly, the narrative implies that high frequency trading arose independently of SEC action, although the agency has been increasingly hyperactive for decades creating the electronic structure we have now, which could not possibly have produced any other result. While some might have naïvely believed that the electronic screens would actually be used for block trading, it has been clear for at least a decade and a half that they were leading to high frequency trading of shredded blocks instead. And regardless of when the scales fell from their eyes, it must be clear by now to even the staunchest NMS advocates that high frequency was caused by NMS. Nonetheless, reporters who fail to follow the SEC's preferred view that high frequency was caused by something other than NMS or the SEC will have trouble with their editors and their sources will dry up. So all articles and opinions on what is wrong with the markets imply that the SEC's view is correct, that the SEC had nothing to do with the problems, and that the problems can only be solved by giving the SEC more power and money and rule-writing authority. No story in the press on any of these issues has mentioned a truth known by everyone in the industry today who is involved in technology, namely, that software testing has been made orders of magnitude more difficult by the high frequency trading the SEC has forced upon the market, to the point that adequate testing is virtually impossible to arrange. Everyone knows, in other words, that all of these glitches and bugs are the SEC's fault, but no one can say it.

After the IPO debacles and the Knightmare, the SEC fulminated about the need to force the culprits (BATS, Nasdaq and Knight) to upgrade their software, and to conform to current rules on software development and testing, and threatened to firm up the Commission's Automation Review Policy (ARP) by making ARP mandatory. [clvi] Like all politically correct views, these remedies sound reasonable to the technically untrained. But even people at the SEC must know they will do no good. To take the most glaring example, the Flash Crash of May 6, 2010 occurred even after three years of live industry trading under the new rules and software the industry had been forced to adopt pursuant to Regulation NMS. This, after much careful testing, with as much coordination as was humanly feasible, and as prudent and slow a rollout as possible – all of it overseen thoroughly and with unprecedented attention to detail by the SEC and industry groups formed specifically for the purpose. Still, the Flash Crash occurred with all due surprise, the markets suddenly overwhelmed by the toxic interaction of stub quotes and stop loss orders under Reg. NMS. [clvii]

While firms can and do conduct extensive quality assurance simulations under artificial computer-generated conditions, it is impossible to test or even imagine all the conditions that any new software will face when it plugs into the highly complex, fragmented high frequency environment. And it is even more difficult to test or predict how the overall NMS conglomeration of all the firms interacting together will behave in any conditions, much less in all conditions. This is a big problem, for it is precisely the unpredictable reverberations of all the parties and systems and human reactions bouncing off each other when they are connected and trading in new situations that cannot be imagined, much less simulated and tested. These are invariably the causes of the biggest black swan problems, such as the Flash Crash, which was ironically not a computer or software malfunction or glitch at all, as is often alleged, but a failure of human imagination, and a fairly simple one at that. Any of the hundreds of industry technologists or traders or regulators involved in rolling out Reg. NMS could have simply said: Wait a minute – what about stub quotes and stop orders? But no one did. The real glitch is that many now know this, but cannot say it. [clviii]

ARP did not have to go all the way to the Flash Crash or the more recent debacles to be recognized as ineffective, and not because it was not mandatory. As implicitly acknowledged by those who insist the SEC needs more money and resources to keep up with Wall Street, it is highly unlikely that a bureaucracy will ever have the expertise of the industry it oversees, no matter how many smart and experienced people it hires. Certainly firms like BATS, Nasdaq and Knight, which are known for the sophistication of their technologies, and did in fact do extensive pre-rollout testing of the software that caused their debacles, are and will always be miles ahead of the SEC. Current SEC Commissioner Daniel M. Gallagher acknowledged as much on October 2, 2012 when, referring to the SEC's ability to keep up with the industry, he said, "we'll never have enough, we'll never be current enough." [clix]

Moreover, more rules, such as one requiring CEOs to certify that their software is failsafe, as has been proposed, cannot possibly give such firms an even greater incentive to get their software right before rolling it out than they have now.

All three firms suffered massive reputation losses and financial hits as a consequence of their errors. Can anyone seriously imagine that authorizing a few bureaucrats to rummage around in their code or to pile on red tape would have helped them discover their problems? With 20/20 hindsight, everything is obvious. And it is always easy to craft draconian new policies to fight the last war. But it is not possible to create policies that will enable the entire industry to see around corners when millions of messages per second are flying around. It is literally impossible to organize a live, production-environment test or an equivalent non-production "test bed" that would include everyone in the industry, especially since participation is itself a constantly fluctuating and unpredictable factor that, as the Flash Crash proved, critically affects results in the most surprising and un-testable ways. And since the industry, pursuant to NMS, is now effectively a single congealed system, such impossible tests would be the only way to find out ahead of the event or circumstance that will bring it down what that event or circumstance is.

Requiring more automated processes or regulatory oversight across the board at all firms and exchanges, like mandating "kill switches" for new software or operations generally, will only compound the problems we have now. If they are manually operated, they could be too slow to stop runaway errors, because whole bear markets can happen in milliseconds now. But if the kill switches operate automatically, they could themselves cause those instant-bear-market debacles when they kick in automatically. Individual firms and industry working groups are in the best position to determine the most effective combinations of manual and automated means of testing and rolling out new software, and of monitoring and building safeguards and halting mechanisms into their operations. They are also in the best position to imagine and suggest various peer monitoring or drop-copy checks to sync up everyone's records of activity in an ongoing and real-time way that would spot problems timely and resolve them as soon as possible. The SEC has nothing to add here. It has no expertise to contribute, and its incentives are dominated by a counterproductive desire to improve its own image by scapegoating market participants for the SEC's errors and pretending that more power for the Commission will improve things in the future.

All of the SEC's NMS rules, from Reg. NMS itself to the proliferating variety of circuit breakers, amount to effective kill switches that are supposed to automatically and instantly prevent bad trades from happening. In reality, however, these automatic processes are experienced as the very trip wires that are causing the glitches and are becoming the primary worries that technology testing must deal with. Technology experts in the industry are fully aware of these problems and the limitations of regulation to deal with them. But, again, none can say so. All, in fact, seem bound to do the opposite, which is to help the SEC rescue and improve its image by devising new trip wires. No one in the industry, inside or outside the SEC, has any leeway whatsoever to criticize the SEC, even though an honest discussion of its failings is what is needed more than anything else if we want to truly sort things out. The entire regulatory discussion, in other words, has become an effective cover-up organized by and for the SEC.

At the SEC, the cover-up is led from the top by senior officials and is fostered by an apparently dishonest culture, one that eschews candid discussion of anything that would make the agency look bad. Since redistribution via fairness and a level playing field is the sum total of what the agency does, and since that motivation underlies all the problems, that means just about everything of consequence is off limits for candid discussion. It also means that the entire agenda for future regulation is designed to cover up the debacles that have resulted from past regulation by proposing similar new initiatives like ARP, CAT, Large Trader, etc.

The multi-billion dollar CAT, or Consolidated Audit Trail, is unlikely to improve investor confidence as promised. In fact, its very building and existence are likely to remove what little is left of such confidence. Premised on the belief that through better surveillance, CAT will enable the Commission to catch more of the bad actors who are abusing their advantages over public investors, the Commission implies that CAT will help it finally level the playing field between professionals, in this case, HFTs, and average "long term" investors. The flaw in this logic begins with the myth that that goal is either possible or desirable. There is no possible construction of markets that would enable average investors of any kind to compete equally with HFTs at *their* business, any more than in the olden days they could have competed with professional block traders. Even the attempt to create such a condition can only serve to convince investors that they are indeed at an unfair and unnecessary disadvantage, a realization that, by the logic of the level-playing-field story, could and should undermine their confidence. By promoting the pretense of a presumed need to compete with HFTs, the CAT initiative can only give investors the impression that their confidence will not and should not return until, with Commission help, investors can do the impossible and do it well, namely compete with HFTs. That impression itself, while it may make the Commission feel important and necessary, can only undermine the legitimate source of confidence that investors should enjoy today, but don't, namely lower trading costs. [clx]

Creating and operating the ideal audit trail will not be an easy task accomplished without investor participation. Like the complex networks of streets that wend and tangle through the cores of our oldest cities, the means by which brokers now identify their customers are also old, but work. CAT will require the replacement of those old methods with new methods that not only identify a broker's customer adequately for that broker, but would also identify him immediately to regulators, without needing to ask the broker, as can be done now with a little extra time for the inquiry. CAT will require instead that the investor be identifiable instantly and before he trades, and in the exact same way for every broker, exchange and regulator who might want to know, and in a way that penetrates and carries through the multiple layers of intermediation by executing brokers, introducing brokers, step-outs, step-ins, routings and re-routings under Reg. NMS that often occur today to handle a customer's order. Complex as they are, the operating mechanics of today's customer identification methods work behind the scenes and do not generally trouble customers beyond providing their brokers with adequate documentation to open their accounts. The new methods under CAT are almost certain to be far more intrusive, at least initially, as they will require the industry to change over to universal identification methodologies that not only identify normal investors, but will also adequately identify all of the potentially nefarious actors out there, from terrorists to front-running HFTs.

While it is conceivable that the enhancements to airline security methods that have been adopted to identify potentially hijacking terrorists have improved the confidence of flyers, traveling by air is an activity that most people cannot avoid. Treating every customer as a potential terrorist is highly intrusive and inconvenient. But the fact that hijackings have occurred and people have to fly makes most people willing to accept the inconvenience, albeit with some grumbling. Investor confidence is a more delicate flower. Investing in stocks is not something that people have to do; it is an option they can easily do without. But there have never been any reports of terrorists having caused any of the debacles that are so prominently undermining confidence today. And whatever the HFTs are doing, the net effect of their activities has been a beneficial reduction in trading costs to investors and traders of all kinds.

The supposed problem with HFTs, that they have advantages over regular investors, is inherent and inevitable. If properly understood, it is a good thing that HFTs seek and attain such advantages, which means only that the industry is sufficiently robust and active to attract professional liquidity providers to it. HFT is not harmful in any way, nor is the existence of HFTs with advantages, nor are any of their supposedly advantage-taking actions, from manipulation to spoofing to front-running to high levels of cancellations and all the other ways they try to make money that the SEC seeks to expose through CAT. The net effect of it all is low trading costs. Like the normal actions that should be within our rights to the pursuit of happiness that antitrust outlaws, all of the actions that HFTs and market-makers have been accused of are also normal, productive, ethical and within their rights to the pursuit of happiness. By promoting the pretense of a benefit to investors from exposing such actions through CAT and suppressing them, the Commission deprives investors of the confidence they would feel if they saw the market functioning well for them. And it instills in them a lack of confidence for not being able to compete with HFTs, a fool's errand the SEC promotes through CAT. In short, the highly intrusive CAT, which like airline security will require investor help to create, but unlike airline security is needed only because of allegedly great dangers that are in fact not there, will undermine confidence.

The fact that markets are occasionally unstable now, as the glitches demonstrate, is the SEC's fault, not the HFTs fault, as is the fact that they no longer raise much capital. Both of these are the flip side of the trading cost benefit. We should not have been surprised that reducing trading costs by reducing the incomes of capital raisers under NMS has resulted in less capital being raised, nor by the fact that stabilizing the market, as the capital raisers used to do, is no longer being done. But by the same token, we should not fantasize that by ratcheting up the intrusiveness of regulation via CAT we can or will improve confidence.

It is ironic that the SEC is always insisting on the need to do this or that in the interest of a level playing field, since everything it has done since 1975 is in that same interest. By their own measures, therefore, the bureaucrats have failed at their primary self-described mission, and they have done so repeatedly, persistently and in every case. By anyone's measure there is little difference morally, or at least none the Commission has articulated, between the advantages HFTs enjoy today and the advantages the block traders that were eliminated to make way for them had. Both had and will always have advantages over non-professionals. It is a self-serving myth promulgated by a Commission looking for excuses to rearrange things that some new construction of the market can make that difference go away. Since the leaders pushing such myths could not possibly be unaware anymore that the myths are not true, those leaders are either lying or so buried in political correctness that they cannot tell the difference.

The leaders of the SEC must know that for the sake of their own personal ambition and the welfare of the agency, they have been ignoring the harm the National Market System has done to investors and to the United States capital markets. They know, for example, the full extent of the Commission's collaboration with Madoff in designing and launching NMS, and they know it was operating just exactly as they designed it to operate when it came apart in the Flash Crash of May 6, 2010. By fostering a culture of dishonesty to cover the Commission's tracks in such debacles, the SEC is also more broadly contributing to the destruction of America. Since the agency's primary purpose is to engage in level playing field promotion, the dissembling must be seen in the context of a society-wide defense of socialism. To avoid the truth, the focus shifts to new non-issues to regulate, new victimless crimes to prosecute, new phantom demons to imprison.

Network scientists may be able to help, albeit in a new role that no one in the field appears to have considered, namely, by describing or merely speculating on the apparent contradictions between public policy and network science. No one in any field of public policy, and no one, it would appear, in the network science field either, is aware of the potential for network science to challenge conventional wisdom and offer solutions to the most intractable problems facing America today. While fascinating articles and books keep pouring out of the field noting the natural existence of inequality due to rich get richer, for example, there is a deafening silence on the fact that public policies everywhere to redistribute wealth conflict with this natural force. Nowhere is there even passing recognition that the policy to destroy networks in the interest of level playing fields conflicts with the operating mechanics of the universe as revealed by network science.

The silence leads many good authors into probable errors that could at least be flagged for review if scientists were to mention these contradictions. Amy Chua, Mark Buchanan, Albert-Laszlo Barabasi, Brian Arthur, Robert Bork, Malcolm Gladwell, Thomas DiLorenzo, Friedrich Hayek and others have offered fascinating analyses and fresh insights, some of which have been referred to in the present work. But not one of them apparently is aware that network formation even conflicts with public policy, much less that there might be something wrong with that policy as a result. The mathematicians among them (Buchanan, Barabasi, Arthur) focus largely on the surprising existence of network effects and how unusual they appear. Similarly, Malcolm Gladwell, an author with a background as a journalist, has written several best sellers around the unusual or "outlier" character of network effects, sometimes titling his books by one of their terms, as in *The Tipping Point,* or otherwise just describing their strange and ubiquitous effects, as in *Outliers,* without confronting any conflicts between network effects and public policy.

While the seeming anomalies are universally presented by these authors as fascinating, surprising and ubiquitous, the potential for them to conflict with current policies is either not mentioned at all or, as in the case of Brian Arthur, used to justify the stringent application of antitrust. Arthur, as noted in Chapter 4, is one of those scientific advisors offering antitrust regulators support by describing lock-in and other concepts that help them bust monopolies. Although scientists like Arthur are correct on the science, their assumptions about the policy implications of their science are shortsighted. They should open their minds to the possibility that, just because monopolies and lock-in exist, does not necessarily mean they should be suppressed. Network scientists have never acknowledged, much less addressed this possibility.

The gap in thinking has led many authors astray. Bork writes a thorough exegesis of the failures of antitrust and concludes that we need the correct version of antitrust that he sees. Gladwell thinks the Robber Baron cohort was just made up of a few lucky guys that happened to be born at a fortunate time. DiLorenzo, in *How Capitalism Saved America*, makes a full-throated denial defense of the Robber Barons against antitrust charges while defending them for their great works. [clxi] By claiming, with regard to Rockefeller, "None of these facts constitute in any way a sign of a monopoly," DiLorenzo forecloses the possibility of defending what the Robber Barons actually did. He apparently doesn't realize that merely by taking that standard denial defense tack, he implicitly condemns monopolies and monopolization if they do exist, when he could have said instead that Rockefeller's great works happened because he *did* monopolize, not because he didn't. Even Hayek sounds at times like Joel Klein and David Boies going after Bill Gates in his criticism of "aimed discrimination." [clxii]

Amy Chua, while offering few prescriptions for the vengeful horrors she describes, nonetheless occasionally opines in standard PC manner on how, for example, "redistribution institutions almost certainly helped dampen the conflict between market wealth disparities and democratic politics in the industrialized West." [clxiii] And she offers a number of suggestions at the end of *World On Fire* implying that more downward redistribution might temper the atrocities. [clxiv] While these latter suggestions are mostly along the lines of voluntary, but highly visible displays of charity, it is hard to escape the implication that they might work only because they mesh with the politically correct view that spreading the wealth is a moral imperative of society that government should embrace. In other words, even after a most penetrating and outside the box analysis of what is really wrong with the world, Chua can only come up with standard inside the box solutions that are nothing more than continuations and intensifications of the policies that were in place as the horrors unfolded. Chua overlooks the possibility that, so long as redistribution is a presumed moral imperative of society, the anger and atrocities are bound to grow. Once redistribution is assumed, it is never enough, because jealousy at any level of inequality will always incite a sense of righteous entitlement to and demands for more. If demands are not met – and they can never be – then those feelings of righteous entitlement can spill over into revenge that has the seeming moral imprimatur of government policy. Chua thus misses the likelihood that government-mandated redistribution, rather than being a solution, may be the root cause of the atrocities she describes.

One can hardly blame Bork or Hayek for not being familiar with theories from a field that did not achieve wide recognition until the 1990s. Given their expressions of support for at least some forms of antitrust, however, it seems likely that even if they had been familiar with such concepts as lock-in, they too would have fallen for the arguments of scientists like Brian Arthur who used them to buttress antitrust.

But never mind the past. The question going forward is: Can network scientists undertake a fresh examination of their field and its policy implications? Merely addressing or even acknowledging the policy conflict could go a long way toward causing a reexamination of the conventional wisdom that has allowed Western societies to paint themselves into the redistributionist corner. It isn't every day that researchers can speak truth to power just by asking interesting questions. Examples of questions that could be asked are:

- Is redistribution supposed to be part of antitrust, or is it not?
- Is the destruction of network monopolies an intended effect of antitrust, or is it not?
- Did we really mean to destroy the market shares of the New York Stock Exchange and Nasdaq?
- Did we really mean to replace what these exchanges used to do with high frequency trading?
- Do we really want dozens of stock exchanges? Hundreds? Thousands? If so, why? If not, how do we determine what the right number is?
- Why can't the right number be 1, if that is what natural, free market competition leads to?

Scientists who support antitrust should not be allowed to continue to ignore the potential positive side of monopolies just because traditional antitrust theory calls for breaking them up. Just because antitrust blocks first mover advantages, tipping points and lock-in, does not mean its advocates should never have to acknowledge the potential benefits of monopolization, such as standardization, coordination, stable order, the inducement of natural monopoly opportunities for invention or capital, or entrepreneurs, or job creation, or the natural protections against being left stranded in abandoned technologies, or the value of natural order instead of government design.

Above all, if network effects, rich get richer and preferential attachment are now recognized to play such important roles in the operation and organization of nature, is it really appropriate for government to devote so much effort to overturning them? If so, let someone make that case. So far the advocates of antitrust have only fit these network effect concepts into the preexisting antitrust framework, ignoring entirely the far better argument on the other side. Stated simply, that argument is that nature – or Nature's God, as the Founders said – should do the designing and creating instead of bureaucrats.

14. Alone

"AND I ONLY AM ESCAPED ALONE TO TELL THEE"
Job.
-Herman Melville, Epilogue to *Moby Dick*

Although Ishmael was alone at the end of *Moby Dick,* the sole survivor of Captain Ahab's monomaniacal pursuit of the white whale, there were eight survivors of the real life sinking of the *Essex* by whale attack, all of which eventually gave accounts of the event that inspired the final scene in America's greatest novel. But far from being the end, the sinking of the *Essex* was only the beginning of a grueling saga of survival in which seven men who died or agreed to be sacrificed were eaten to extend the lives of their fellow shipmates.

For testing man's courage and morality, nothing compares to shipwreck situations. Whether we have minutes or hours before the ship goes down, or weeks or months on the open sea, nothing tests our ethical protocols, our willingness to share or sacrifice, like the prospect of imminent death for some, but not all of us. Does the captain go down with the ship? Is women-and-children-first honored? Do rich get better treatment than poor? Do some races suffer more? When drawing lots to see who will be sacrificed and eaten to save others, do all agree the process was fair, and will the loser accept his fate because it was? While not everyone measures up to our ideal in such tests, some do and are favorably remembered. In any case, we know what the ideal is, and personal ambition is out of place. When you and your neighbor are about to meet God, it is just not right to seek one last advantage.

Fortunately, shipwreck situations are rare. While dealing with one makes it clear that shared sacrifice is sometimes called for, ordinarily the better way to relieve scarcity is to find or create more resources. Here ambition can play a big role. Moreover, provided it is pursued with respect for the right of others to do the same, the freedom of each of us to pursue our own happiness can produce great material abundance as well as good morals and clear consciences. While we Americans have faltered in our attachment to freedom of late, we originally embraced it deliberately, grasping the nettle of inequality and discovering a path to riches no king could imagine. Alone among nations, America provided the moral and practical framework for ambition to turn the work of men into miracles that spread their benefits to all mankind.

Few better examples exist than the history of illumination. From fire to torches to candles, the resource known as light had been refined and expanded by various means over the millennia. The discovery that sperm-whale oil produced candles that burned "longer and brighter than any in the world" [clxv] provided the germ for one such advance. In a pre-Declaration demonstration of the value of religious liberty, the entrepreneurial Quakers of Nantucket turned devotion to God in their close-knit community on a tiny island of sand into *the* engine of prosperity for early America. Dedicating themselves to perfecting the hunt and processing methods for these most dangerous but most valuable whales, they pioneered the use of arduous, long and perilous voyages, going far beyond the shorter trips and easier hunts the rest of the whaling world was satisfied with. Through thrift, courage and persistence, Nantucket locked in a global sperm-whale illumination monopoly from the mid-eighteenth to the mid-nineteenth century that included everything from financing and outfitting whaling voyages to making candles in over 35 factories. By the time the baton was passed to New Bedford [clxvi] and other mostly American whaling towns, America dominated the world of whaling, supplying a resource that enabled humans to light the night and expand their lives. So great was the demand for this improvement that sperm-whale populations were dwindling fast by the middle of the nineteenth century, [clxvii] causing ships to extend voyages out to six years, and even then to often come back without filling their holds. [clxviii]

But soon after Melville wrote *Moby Dick* (1851) and Marx and Engels wrote *The Communist Manifesto* (1848), an even better source of illumination was discovered: oil (1859 in Titusville, Pennsylvania). And again, the physical discovery wasn't the half of it, as John D. Rockefeller turned thrift and persistence into riches. Within a couple of decades, by standardizing under Standard Oil what had previously been a dangerously inconsistent kerosene product provided by a variety of suppliers, and by steadily reducing its price from 30 cents to 8 cents a gallon through superior production and delivery networks, [clxix] Rockefeller locked in a vertically and horizontally integrated illumination monopoly that provided an even better and cheaper source of light than sperm-whale oil.

Then in 1878, Thomas Edison hooked up with financier and monopolist J. P. Morgan to create what became General Electric, producing light bulbs and the electricity to keep them on, an even better and cheaper source of light than kerosene. And again, for all the inventive genius of Edison, it was the rapid and powerful organization of the delivery of these products through General Electric that was primarily responsible for spreading their benefits to America and beyond.

Throughout our history, Americans have invented and commercialized through monopolization industry after industry, from the examples above to railroads, steel, automobiles, air travel, telecommunication, TV, even movies, not to mention the stock exchanges that facilitated raising capital for them all. There is nothing like America, not even close in the modern age or any age, for inspiring and allowing man to make the most of his world.

As mentioned, the Robber Barons created the greatest fortunes in world history. [clxx] But they didn't just create wealth for themselves with their "trusts." Their success ignited and drove the rapid growth of the wealth of their nation, too.

During the 1870s and 1880s, the U. S. economy rose at the fastest rate in its history, with real wages, wealth, GDP and capital formation all increasing rapidly. [clxxi] For example, between 1865 and 1898, the output of wheat increased by 256%, corn by 222%, coal by 800% and miles of railway track by 567%. [clxxii] Thick national networks for transportation and communication were created. The corporation became the dominant form of business organization, and a managerial revolution transformed business operations. [clxxiii] By the beginning of the 20th century, per capita income and industrial production in the United States led the world, with per capita incomes double that of Germany or France, and 50% higher than Britain. [clxxiv]

Unfortunately, the trusts created by the likes of Rockefeller, Carnegie and Morgan, were snuffed out by the Sherman Antitrust Act of 1890. Since the Progressive Era kicked off by Theodore Roosevelt and the Sherman Act, Americans have been told to pretend our resources are shrinking, as if they were fixed daily rations nibbled away by starving men on a battered boat. Our politics has devolved into nothing but deciding whose rations to cut and which men to sacrifice. Demagogues build careers on our fears, claiming they can do miracles themselves with "infrastructure spending" and designs born in Washington. They can't and never could. But as a result of their never ending attempts to do the impossible, the real infrastructure, the industrial backbone of America that was built by monopolizing geniuses, is going to seed, not only not replaced but destroyed by bureaucrats who think they know better.

Politicians claim to know what the American people want, and exhort us to follow them as they pretend to statesmanlike compromise on "common ground." None is honest enough to admit there can be no common ground when the only issue that matters is redistribution. Either it will tilt upward a little for the next four years as, say, Obamacare is repealed and right wing social engineers take over, or it will tilt downward a bit as Obamacare is retained and left wing engineers dominate a while longer. But either way there will be no common ground. A very large minority, almost certainly somewhere between 40% and 49% of the people, will hate and fear the situation, view it as theft and redistribution of their property, and work to overturn it four years hence. Politicians who use "common ground" to describe such razor-thin and temporary majorities, are by definition dishonest.

The one substantive domestic issue on which there is true common ground is antitrust. Liberals believe monopolies should be busted to break up their price-fixing conspiracies and spread their wealth to the masses. Conservatives say they don't care about redistribution, but believe monopolies should be busted anyway in order to address "inefficiency." The details of their arguments amount to complex theoretical nonsense. [clxxv] But their agreement on common ground to bust all monopolies results in the perpetual prevention of America's ever again achieving the brilliant economic performance of its past.

The one substantive international issue on which there is common ground is that the War On Terror must be fought and won, a consensus that alone should make us wary of common ground. This undeclared "war" against a behavior of an enemy we can't even name without paragraphs of softening explanations, has caused nothing but loss of blood and treasure with nothing to show for it. An honest assessment would reveal that both the threat and the war itself are self-generating consequences of waging it, apparitions that would disperse overnight if we dropped the policy. But because the opposing party would block such honesty as unpatriotic or treasonous, there is little chance of challenging this consensus.

And there is an even bigger reason to worry: what politicians call common ground is often a steppingstone to a killing field. Hitler's Germany found common ground on the need to rid the world of Jews, Rwandans on the need to kill Tutsis,

Serbs on the need to kill Muslims and, unfolding in South Africa now, black majorities on the need to cleanse the land of white farmers in order to redistribute their property. Once the unalienables start to go, with compromises to property and the pursuit of happiness, eventually life and liberty will go, too. It doesn't matter that there may be very large minorities, or even hidden majorities opposing such policies. In fear of mobs chanting on common ground, people of conscience can be readily intimidated into the shadows as the violence unfolds. Things are bound to go wrong when government, instead of protecting the naturally equal rights of everyone, contrives to grant special rights and special protections and special advantages to some groups over others.

We once thought our theory of government and history of freedom in America would protect us from such errors. But in Redistributionist America, that is no longer true. Every single issue driving voters to the polls in our 2012 election is a redistribution issue, either directly or by proxy as an identifier of group allegiance on redistribution. And no matter what the outcome, after it is over, very nearly half the country is going to be angry and frightened, at least for their economic welfare.

We have managed to convince ourselves that redistribution to certain broad classes is wise and moral policy, particularly if it is styled as reparations for past harm. So we undertake affirmative actions and new civil rights to promote the aggrieved, including now the middle class and the 99%. This can only be done at the expense of those in the 1% whose rights are abridged for redistribution purposes. Doing so harms both those individuals and the potential for society to benefit from their capabilities, which is no small loss, since they are far and away its most productive members. They are the ones who organize, who give purpose and meaning to labor, who provide jobs. They are the traditional wellspring of America's wealth, and the only ones who can address the fixed and frightening scarcities the politicians have fashioned for us.

Meanwhile, like Hitler and like Ahab, our leaders are just waiting for their moment. Their lackeys apply fevered formulas to determine the proper number of stock exchanges and airlines and phone companies and banks, [clxxvi] and the proper percentages of various groups in various occupations, their judgments guiding righteous redistribution to offset grievances or disadvantages or current or past discrimination. And we listen rapt as they conjure up malevolent forces for us to fight, leading us to revenge that will eventually take us down with them.

Stopping the further progress of such monomaniacs is a challenge, but if anyone can do it, it would be us. We do know the formula. Maximizing human interaction, as occurs naturally under the pursuit of happiness, is the best way – time-tested and proved here in America – to create and enjoy more of what life has to offer. As economists from Smith to Ricardo to Mises have said, pursuing what we want to do, and keeping the fruits of our labor, is the way to find our own and our country's comparative advantage. It is the way to maximize the amount we have to share, and to figure out the most efficient and the fairest way of sharing it. It will tell us the right balance between rich and poor, and give everyone the opportunity to contribute and earn a livelihood to the best of their ability. Natural and unfettered human interaction is the only reliable way to tell us the right number of stock exchanges or the right balance of women and men in various roles and occupations, or for that matter, of minorities, gays, lesbians, homosexuals and transgendered individuals. Everyone has something to add to the human endeavor, and natural and unfettered human interaction is the one and only way to find out what it is.

Our Founders said as much in our Declaration of Independence when they said our right to the pursuit of happiness is unalienable. While governments, demagogues and monomaniacs may temporarily block our use of it – it's still there. If we can only summon the will to resist today's tyranny, we could relearn how to exercise our right to the pursuit of happiness. But if we fail to muster the courage, there is every indication that our decline as a civilization and as a nation will continue and accelerate, led by the ongoing disintegration of our stock market.

On September 14, 2012 the SEC hit the NYSE with a first-ever-for-an-exchange fine of $5 million for not being sufficiently attentive to the potential for some people to get their market data before others, a result that is guaranteed in any case and in every case in the high frequency mayhem the SEC has created. Fining exchanges for falling into traps the Commission has itself set is bold beyond belief. Even the Inquisition didn't go that far. [clxxvii]

Meanwhile, many industry experts are calling for an urgent review of the rules the Commission put in place in 2007. The Regulation NMS rule that forced automation, fragmentation and high frequency trading on the NYSE beginning in 2007 was virtually identical in its effect to the automation, fragmentation and high frequency trading that had been visited on Nasdaq a decade earlier by the Order Handling rules. Thus no one should have been surprised by this result, although now many are acting as if they were surprised, probably out of a combination of politically correct deference to the SEC and fear for their careers. Although it must be obvious to many of these experts that the SEC is the cause of all of these problems associated with high frequency trading, the bravest and most candid of them can still only bring themselves to call timidly for a "holistic" approach this time, as one NYSE official did. [clxxviii] No one can acknowledge that the SEC is the problem and that, therefore, no solution is possible as long as the SEC remains in control of stock market structure and regulation. Because of such timidity, the SEC is on track to remain firmly in charge of its destiny, and ours, at least as to how our economic fortunes are affected by the capital markets. Any reassessments of the situation organized by the Commission will only grant the Commission greater power and authority as it pushes us further down into the depths of dysfunction and disrepair.

Congressional overseers of the Commission are aiding and abetting the Commission's drive for more power, ostensibly in efforts to engage in and be part of those holistic reassessments. Senator Jack Reed, on CNBC the morning of the September 20th 2012 hearings his committee was holding into high frequency trading, vowed to grant the Commission any further legislative authority it needed. Senator Reed wanted to make sure we never again have another Flash Crash, BATS, Facebook or Knightmare. But no one posed the obvious question: Since the United States Congress has been granting the SEC ever more legislative authority since the National Market System was authorized thirty-seven years ago, why would more authority now solve the problems that have been springing up all along under NMS, problems that never existed before?

It takes no clairvoyance or genius to predict the obvious outcome of the SEC's and Congress's hyperactive legislative and regulatory attentions. Merely extrapolating from the past, in type, frequency and severity of debacles, paints a picture of ever-greater debacles in our future, ones that, as with those just mentioned, will be caused by the SEC's electronic trip wires. New preventative measures will again be styled as efficiency or stability measures, but will again just create more trip wires under lulling euphemisms like "circuit breakers" or "level playing fields." In the current atmosphere, perhaps "ball-and-chains" for high frequency traders in the form of market-making obligations or slowed down trading would seem appropriate. None of these will work to improve market structure. clxxix In fact, it is highly likely based on past performance that such measures will only accelerate the flood of distrustful and confused investors fleeing the market, and will lead to ever more frequent and violent debacles. The SEC's highest priority initiatives to make sure that a Flash Crash never again happens will be either embarrassingly error prone and unnecessary, as the stand-in "single stock circuit breakers" quickly fashioned for that purpose have been, or will, like Reg. NMS, do new and surprising harm.

Heightened oversight tools like CAT meant to make the Commission look good and the industry look bad and dangerous will only succeed in making the industry look bad and dangerous as its processes are put under a regulatory microscope. In this vein, the latest resident evil is a shadowy order type called Hide Not Slide, which one "reformed" high frequency trader apparently didn't know about until someone at a Christmas party held by an exchange let him in on the secret in a casual conversation. clxxx While this lack of fair and timely disclosure, in the trader's view, caused him to lose or not make as much money high frequency trading, glossed over is that the rule, like all rules, is required to be disclosed in public documents and approved by the SEC.

Also glossed over is that Hide Not Slide is but one of many accommodations that an exchange is bound to develop to deal with the requirements of transparency and routing under Reg. NMS. Since the SEC bans the display of orders that would "lock" or "cross" the other side (conditions that occur when a new bid to buy is displayed that is equal to or higher priced than the best visible offer to sell in the combination of all markets in the National Market System), an HFT who wants his order to only be displayed and then *taken from the book* of the market through which he originally entered the NMS (so he can earn a liquidity rebate as a "maker" of liquidity there), as opposed to being a *taker of an order from another book* after routing to that other market pursuant to Reg. NMS, may want to use Hide Not Slide. To avoid locking or crossing situations, the SEC interpreted Reg. NMS to require non-displayable orders to either 1) be routed to whatever other NMS market had the best still-available "protected" clxxxi displayed other side order when the non-displayable order was placed, or 2) be canceled back un-displayed to the order placer, or 3) be slid in price to a less aggressive price where it would not lock or cross the other side and can thus be legally displayed, or 4) be held un-displayed at the exchange ("hidden") until conditions change. Thus Hide Not Slide is actually short for Hide Not Route Not Cancel Not Slide. The HFT market maker uses this order type because of a number of reasons related to his desire to avoid the effect of

Reg. NMS. First, becoming a taker and paying the liquidity fee at the routed-to market (some of which goes to the maker there) would defeat his purpose of making money as a maker at his original market. Second, he usually would see no opportunity as a maker at the less aggressive but legally displayable price to which his order could slide. Third, sliding to it would take him out of the running to be a maker at his original price as soon as that was legally permissible, which is probably still his goal. So he would rather bide his time and wait until conditions change by *not* placing his order for the time being on the displayed book at all. He could do this in a couple of ways. He could effectively hide it either by taking the canceled order back himself and waiting and watching for conditions to change and then replacing it by placing a new order just like it, or he could leave it with the exchange to hide it for him, and watch and wait for him, too. He usually wouldn't want to do the watching and waiting himself by having his order canceled back to him, as that would make him have to start over and, equally important, would miss out on the better strategy of having the market itself make the judgment of when the order will be legally displayable again, something it is in a better position to do than he is, because it has faster access certainly to its own prices and perhaps to those of other markets, too. In addition, since it has the order already, the routing time to send it back to the exchange to put in the book is much shorter. So the market itself is in a far better position to carry out his order placement strategy from that point than the trader is, and he therefore chooses Hide Not Slide. That way he can be the first on the book or at least near the front of the queue the instant he can legally show his order, and be a market-making bidder at his original price. It is only natural under this circumstance for an exchange to offer tools and order types that can do these kinds of things automatically for high frequency traders. Since prices can change multiple times per second as an order is being entered, only machines run by algorithms can operate effectively in this market, not humans. Running on slow human time would certainly fail to achieve the above described order placement goals and therefore would force the market maker to drop out of the market-making business at that exchange, if it didn't have order types like Hide Not Slide. And, as discussed in Chapter 3, exchanges that fail to attract high frequency traders will die for lack of liquidity. If they want to survive, exchanges have no choice but to develop rules and order types like Hide Not Slide, at least for high frequency traders. The existence of these kinds of orders, which are similar in effect to the most popular order type at the NYSE, called DNS, or Do Not Ship (i.e., do not send my order away to another exchange) is proof that traders of every stripe are skeptical of the efficiency benefits of Reg. NMS with all of its routing-to-best-price requirements. These orders simply say "skip all that and leave me at the exchange where I entered my order."

If you found this description difficult to understand, welcome to NMS. If you think average investors can compete with high frequency traders, good luck. If you think investors *should* be able to compete with them, you have bought into the SEC's self-serving propaganda implying that consumers of a service should be equal to professional providers of that service, in this case the provision of market liquidity. The quixotic attempt to equalize these two fundamentally and irretrievably unequal market participant types is at the heart of the SEC's four-decade mission to level the playing field, an attempt that has produced only confusion, chaos and escalating complaints of inequality. A dispassionate analysis of the level playing field would expose it as the central catechism of an incoherent belief system, one that, like all Marxist and messianic spread-the-wealth systems of the past, will not and cannot actually achieve its goals. The level playing field is so fervently believed in not in spite of its incoherence, but because of its incoherence. As with all such systems, it is a *religious* belief in the righteousness of a cause, not the result of rational analysis that its advocates claim.

High frequency traders should not be blamed for any of these problems, from flash crashes to the dearth of IPOs. Neither market stability nor raising capital is in their wheelhouse. The problem is that markets are now reliant for liquidity and over half of all trading on high frequency traders who cannot fulfill these functions. That is our problem. But it is not their fault. No holistic solutions in hearings or roundtables or studies or comment periods will solve it, no matter how transparent and public-spirited they are. The rising chorus of calls for urgent reviews of market structure are understandable, but off the mark. The chaos is clearly accelerating, but it is not occurring because of the lack of reviews or discussions, holistic or otherwise. It is occurring because of such reviews and discussions, which are expert-driven efforts to design markets from the top down orchestrated by the SEC, and they have been underway for four decades. This is the essence of redistributive socialism, and it is what the SEC does. But the level playing field is farther away than ever.

> Order types have proliferated into the thousands in recent years, making it difficult for institutional traders and other market participants to keep up with all the choices and their appropriate usage. Many are targeted, as well, at high-speed, automated traders . . . BATS Global Markets alone has more than 2,000 order types in use, according to its chief operating officer, Chris Isaacson. Some trading execs – on both the buyside and the sellside – have complained that is too many. The beef is that their sheer numbers add undue complexity to the marketplace. Also, there is a concern that certain order types give advantages to some traders over others. [clxxxii]

All of the complex, confusing and shadowy-seeming order types introduced in recent times were devised in response to Reg. NMS and primarily seek to avoid its goals and intent. Since these mandated automatic best price routing goals and intent have been the core mechanism of the National Market System since 1975, and are the vehicle by which it will allegedly deliver the level playing field, investors' reactions to the new order types are very relevant. The popularity of order types like Hide Not Slide and DNS means that investors and traders are voting with their feet to avoid the SEC's chaotic creation, and will do so whenever they understand how it works and such order types well enough to use them. What those who are calling for reviews of market structure don't realize is that such discussions organized by the SEC are how we got into the mess we are in today. More discussion will only make matters worse. These problems are endemic to NMS and the SEC's oversight of it, and will not go away until the SEC and NMS go away.

The tendency to greater chaos is accelerating all around us. In terms of international relations among peoples, this means not just weird stock prices, but violence. The same philosophies and theories inspiring the SEC are also inspiring a Western crusade of global conquest. Like all such crusades, if continued it will certainly collapse, and almost certainly amidst thousands or millions of deaths. We should in fact *expect* chaos, since it is policy everywhere in the West to block or kill the network-formation process that creates order, that organizes chaos and makes it less chaotic. It may seem counterintuitive that the best way to create order is to leave nature alone, but that's the way it is. That is why America's Founders declared our unalienable right to the pursuit of happiness, which is first and foremost a right to be left alone to pursue our interests free of government control or coercion.

And that is why modern network science often goes under names like "emergence," "complexity" and other labels suggesting the beautiful structures that network processes naturally produce if left free to work their wonders. Critical to both the Founders' faith in the laws of nature and of nature's God, and the laws that network scientists are discovering today, is that the most beautiful, complex, structured, orderly and wonderful patterns can emerge only if we stand back and observe, in awe, what natural and free interactions can create. We don't know *and cannot know ahead of time* what those structures will look like. But we must nonetheless trust that freedom will produce better results than deliberate design could produce. Government intervention, in particular, mostly just gets in the way. In the long run, intervention can only lead to relative disorder and chaos, because it upsets the natural interactions of a free people that would otherwise produce order. The Founders did not need network scientists to tell them these truths about freedom. But we do need them today to help us better understand what the Founders were trying to tell us.

Endnotes

[i] United States Declaration of Independence, July 4, 1776.

[ii] *NEXUS: SMALL WORLDS and the Groundbreaking SCIENCE OF NETWORKS.* Mark Buchanan, W. W. Norton & Company, New York, 2002, Amazon Kindle, 2003, Kindle location 720.

[iii] *Growing Income Inequality in OECD Countries: What Drives It and How Can Policy Tackle It?* Office of Economic Cooperation and Development Forum, Paris, May 2, 2011. In Figure 5, "Market incomes are distributed much more unequally than net incomes," every country for which the OECD has data shows inequality. The United States has more inequality than all major countries. www.oecd.org/els/social/inequality/.

[iv] *Millionaires Control 39% of Global Wealth*, Robert Frank, The Wall Street Journal, October 19, 2011.

[v] *Concern in GOP Over State Focus on Social Issues,* Michael Cooper, The New York Times, April 21, 2012. Tennessee Governor Bill Haslam used this phrase referring to the rise of social issues in the 2012 elections.

[vi] *The Paradox of the New Elite*, Alexander Stille, The New York Times, October 22, 2011.

[vii] OECD has a $342 million budget funded by its 34 members in proportion to the relative size of their economies. The United States is the largest and pays 24% of the OECD budget. www.oecd.org.

[viii] *Growing Income Inequality in OECD Countries: What Drives It and How Can Policy Tackle It?* Office of Economic Cooperation and Development Forum, Paris, May 2, 2011. Final section: "Have income taxes and benefit systems become less effective at redistributing income?" www.oecd.org/els/social/inequality/.

[ix] "Today's income disparities are global in scope – at historic extremes in state-directed socialist systems such as China, as well as in market-based capitalist systems of the west." *A Veteran Wall-Streeter confronts the Occupy movement*, Stephen Roach, Morgan Stanley Asia and Yale, Financial Times, January 30, 2012.

[x] Personal note: I live in the area.

[xi] 60 Minutes, CBS, December 11, 2011.

[xii] The attack began formally on May 1, 1975 with the implementation of the National Market System Amendments, Section 11A, to the Securities Exchange Act of 1934. On Wall Street, this day is known as Mayday, and resulted among other things in the prohibition of fixed commissions, thus beginning the "deregulation" of the industry by forcing it to adhere to antitrust dictates. The most serious updates to 11A and deregulation/antitrust dictates came with the 1996 Order Handling rules, implemented in 1997, and the 2005 Regulation NMS "trade through" rule, implemented in 2007. The first of these forced automation and high frequency trading on Nasdaq listed stocks, while the second forced automation and high frequency trading on NYSE listed stocks. The rules had their intended antitrust effects of decimating their respective markets' dominant market shares, each of which went from over 80% to under 25% in short order.

[xiii] If the Occupiers want to find out where their jobs went, they should start here: *Market Structure Is Causing the IPO Crisis – and more*; Grant Thornton Capital Markets Series paper by David Weild and Edward Kim; June, 2010.

[xiv] *Buy Low Sell High? Not In This Market*, David Weidner, The Wall Street Journal, April 12, 2012.

[xv] *On Wall Street, the Rising Cost of Faster Trades,* Nathaniel Popper, New York Times, August 13, 2012.

[xvi] *The Antitrust Paradox: A Policy at War With Itself*, Robert H. Bork, Basic Books, New York, 1978, pp 110-112. Purists say antitrust is only about efficiency, not redistribution. In practice, the wealth-spreading goals are usually taken up and emphasized by the Blue Team, while the Red Team champions the efficiency goals. The main methods of redress for accomplishing both goals are the same and therefore afford the two teams a rare opportunity to agree wholeheartedly on policy. But their public agreement, while solidifying political support for antitrust to virtually 100%, masks a rotten foundation because these diametrically opposite theories – in support of redistribution or opposed to redistribution – underlie the same policy goals.

[xvii] See *Nexus*, by Mark Buchanan, on electric utilities and airlines (Kindle location 2009-2021). In addition, many other troubled components of United States infrastructure are at least saddled with similar spread-the-wealth policies and, one must assume, may be suffering from similar network-crippling effects. These would include policies as ancient as the universal service of our post office and, in more recent times, our no-child-left-behind education policies, as well as attempts to create or maintain universal coverage in health insurance and telecommunications.

[xviii] Dictum Meum Pactum is the motto of the modern Security Traders Association and was also the motto of traders going back to the nineteenth century London Stock Exchange. I discussed the value of Dictum Meum Pactum to capital formation and other ethics-based functions of capital markets, and the cost of its loss under NMS in *Dark Pool Comment Letter*, Amazon Kindle, 2010, Kindle location 458-525. The letter is also available on the SEC's website at http://www.sec.gov/comments/s7-27-09/s72709-32.pdf

[xix] *Letter to SEC Chairman Mary Schapiro*, Congressman Darrell Issa, Chairman, House Oversight and Government Reform Committee, March 22, 2011. I discuss the situation further at the beginning of *War on Wealth: The SEC, the National Market System and the Flash Crash,* Steve Wunsch, Amazon Kindle, May 2, 2011, Kindle location 4.

[xx] *War on Wealth: The SEC, the National Market System and the Flash Crash,* Steve Wunsch, Amazon Kindle, May 2, 2011, Kindle location 21.

[xxi] Ranging from honesty (my word is my bond) to size of capital to number of trusted counterparties, *fitness* to survive in a Darwinian sense was a constant factor as each party was judged by others and accepted or rejected by them.

[xxii] Shortly after the Order Handling rules forced the splintering of the Nasdaq market (1996-1997), the options markets were also pushed by the SEC to adopt antitrust-based reforms requiring them to abandon previous "gentleman's agreements" amounting to a per se antitrust violation called "market division" in

which there was only one market for the trading of options on each equity security. Now there are many options exchanges for all the options and their number is growing, as old markets launch clones and new ones are launched from scratch, just as in equities. Although the mechanics and structure are somewhat different, the same high frequency environment that pertains in equities is causing a great proliferation of data in options, too, particularly because for each price change of an underlying stock there may be hundreds of needed price changes in the quotations of the options on that stock. Quote to trade ratios are in the twenties in stocks, but over five thousand in options and, as in equities, most of those quotations must be disseminated, in this case via the Options Price Reporting Authority (OPRA).

xxiii The record per second rate as of October 18, 2012 was 6.65 million messages on October 7, 2011. Financial Information Forum, Exegy: MarketDataPeaks.com.

xxiv The Markets in Financial Instruments Directive (MiFID) is a competition policy of the European Union pushing regulatory harmonization across its 30 member states.

xxv *New Canadian Trade-At Rule Gets Mixed Reviews,* John D'Antona Jr., Traders Magazine, May 15, 2012.

xxvi *Trading Error Jolts India Index,* Gurdev Singh, Ashutosh Joshi, The Wall Street Journal, October 5, 2012. "The push for greater scrutiny comes as regulators and investors across three continents fret over the recent dominance of high-frequency traders, which often profit from paper-thin differences in stock prices, and the role their computer programs may have played in some of the most frantic moments since the financial crisis. The National Stock Exchange said Friday that its systems functioned normally, and the decline in the index was due to orders that resulted in multiple trades at low prices. The trades triggered a circuit breaker, a trading band that, if breached, causes an automatic halt in trading, the National Stock Exchange said in a statement."

xxvii These markets are by no means immune to the pressures to fragment their markets, too: *When Fragmentation Comes to Brazil*, TabbForum.com, Alice Botis, Fidessa, March 27, 2012.

xxviii This at least is the story often told by those who like to emphasize government's role in the Internet's creation. Others have disputed this account: *Who Really Invented the Internet? Contrary to legend, it wasn't the federal government, and the Internet had nothing to do with maintaining communications during a war,* L. Gordon Crovitz, Wall Street Journal, July 22, 2012.

xxix Letter to Jonathan G. Katz, Secretary, U.S. Securities & Exchange Commission from R. Steven Wunsch, President, AZX, September 15, 1997, Re: Concept Release: Regulation of Exchanges; Rule ATS, Release No. 34-38672, International Series Release No. 1S-1085; File No. S7-16-97. The letter is also in *Auction Countdown*, Steve Wunsch, Amazon Kindle, 2010, Kindle location 4988. The referenced section is at Kindle location 5101.

xxx *War on Wealth: The SEC, the National Market System and the Flash Crash,* Steve Wunsch, Amazon Kindle, 2011, Kindle location 276.

xxxi Prolific mathematician Leonhard Euler gave birth to graph theory in 1736 by solving the Königsberg Bridge problem, a puzzle that had amused residents of the town near St. Petersburg until Euler proved it was impossible. He illustrated his proof by representing the land areas as points, or nodes, and the bridges as links between them, creating the first "graph." *Linked: The New Science of Networks*, Albert-Laszlo Barabasi, Perseus Publishing, Amazon Kindle, 2002, Kindle location 224-285.

xxxii Apart from Pareto, who saw around 1900 that 80% of the peas were in 20% of the pods, there were other precursors to this line of thinking. Derek de Solia Price observed power laws in citation networks in 1965, and in 1976 suggested that *cumulative advantage*, a term similar in meaning to preferential attachment, caused the phenomenon. Harvard linguist George Kingsley Zipf proposed what became known as *Zipf's law* in 1935 and 1949, which held that the frequency of words used in language was inversely proportional to their rank in terms of frequency, in other words, exhibited a power law distribution. French stenographer Jean-Baptiste Estoup noted the same relationship even earlier, in 1912. And in 1913 Felix Auerbach saw it in the rankings of cities by their populations. In spite of these sporadic early sightings, a critical mass of researchers did not emerge to fully flesh out preferential attachment until the 1990s and especially around 2000, with new research by Albert-Laszlo Barabasi and associates. Wikipedia. Some of this history, as well as Barabasi's and his associates' findings are described in *Linked: The New Science of Networks*, Albert-Laszlo Barabasi, Perseus Publishing, Amazon Kindle, 2002.

xxxiii *The Antitrust Paradox: A Policy at War with Itself,* Robert H. Bork, Basic Books, Inc. 1978, p. 26.

xxxiv *Increasing Returns and Path Dependence in the Economy,* W. Brian Arthur, The University of Michigan Press, 1994, p. 10. "Increasing-returns mechanisms do not merely tilt competitive balances among nations; they can also cause economies – even such successful ones as the United States and Japan – to become locked into inferior paths of development. A technology that improves slowly at first but that has enormous long-term potential could easily be shut out, locking an economy into a path that is both inferior and difficult to escape."

xxxv *Increasing Returns and Path Dependence in the Economy,* W. Brian Arthur, The University of Michigan Press, 1994, p. 12. "Steering an economy with positive feedbacks into the best of its many possible equilibrium states requires good fortune and good timing – a feel for the moments when beneficial change from one pattern to another is most possible. Theory can help identify these states and times, and it can guide policymakers in applying the right amount of effort (not too little but not too much) to dislodge locked-in structures."

xxxvi A senior SEC regulator in the Division of Market Regulation (which has since changed its name to the Division of Trading & Markets) describes how these relatively modern and unfamiliar network effect theories translate into the SEC's current NMS policy. In a paper that, as always, disclaims any connection to the SEC or anyone working there, but nonetheless accurately articulates the policy, he lays the groundwork by correctly noting via a rhetorical question that, based on network effect theory, competition among exchanges is likely to collapse to a single exchange without regulation preventing that result: "First, given the powerful network effect that operates in the equity markets – best captured in the old maxim that liquidity attracts liquidity – is significant competition among equity markets for trading volume in the same stocks likely to exist in the absence of a regulatory scheme that makes such competition a primary objective?" Clearly, he implies, the answer is no. He then applies this insight to the current situation as follows: "The consequences of the network effect can be seen today by assessing the equity markets throughout the world. The network effect appears to be alive and well. In countries other than the U.S., the major equity exchanges overwhelmingly dominate public trading in their listed stocks. Examples include the LSE in the United Kingdom; the Tokyo Stock Exchange in Japan; Deutsche Börse in Germany; Euronext in France, the Netherlands, Belgium and Portugal; and the Toronto Stock Exchange in Canada. In contrast, the U.S. equity markets currently are characterized by extremely vigorous competition among a variety of different types of markets for trading volume in the same stocks." Note the author's apparent pride in the fact that America's SEC is ahead of the word's other stock market regulators in breaking up their dominant incumbents, a situation that, as I noted in Chapter 3, is rapidly changing as the other regulators follow the SEC's lead. The author concludes with a ringing endorsement of current policy as embodied in Reg. NMS: "In adopting Regulation NMS, the Commission concluded that the market structure for both NYSE and Nasdaq stocks would be improved – *though in different ways that reflect their current structural differences* – by an updated and strengthened trade-through rule that protects only those displayed quotations that are immediately and automatically accessible. The SEC noted that the new rule would promote competition by new or smaller markets with larger markets by assuring the markets that, if they display the best prices, they will attract order flow and cannot simply be ignored by participants in dominant markets." [Emphasis added]. I italicize the "structural differences" part of this concluding passage to highlight the fact that the result of its ministrations has been far different from what the SEC expected. Not only are there no longer any meaningful structural differences between the markets, as they are now all virtual clones of each other, but the hopeful talk of the value of competition has given way to defending fragmentation and its main consequence, high frequency trading, both of which have reached levels of intensity that were not anticipated. *THE ESSENTIAL ROLE OF REGULATION IN PROMOTING EQUITY MARKET COMPETITION,* Daniel M. Gray, Senior Special Counsel for Market Structure, Division of Market Regulation, U.S. Securities and Exchange Commission. The paper appears to have been written in 2007 or 2008.

xxxvii *Countdown,* Steve Wunsch, 2001, Amazon Kindle, 2010, Kindle location 1070-1105.

xxxviii NYSE and the other "regional" exchanges had been forced to compete with each other for best price in the NYSE's list of stocks in the 1980s under NMS's first iteration, the "Intermarket Trading System," or ITS. Because ITS involved sending messages to specialists at other exchanges that required physical human responses before trading through them, the system was not automatic or immediate, a situation that Reg. NMS, implemented in 2007, was directed to address. Although Nasdaq became a member of ITS for the purpose of competing with exchanges for best price in exchange-listed stocks, the OTC list of Nasdaq had its own brand of competition in the form of multiple competing dealers, which was also not automatic or immediate, a situation the Order Handling rules implemented in 1997 were directed to address. The Nasdaq dealer market for OTC stocks, i.e., Nasdaq stocks before Nasdaq became an exchange, was distinct from ITS's mechanism and not included in it. Over the years it became easier and easier for partisans of each market to criticize the other for its method of competition and claim that it was inconsistent with the National Market System, largely because neither of them were, as described, automatic or immediate under the first pass at NMS's electronic vision. The SEC generally went along with such criticism and eventually busted them both, requiring fully electronic and immediate execution of all orders, as all exchanges, including NYSE and Nasdaq, do today.

xxxix *Auction Countdown*, Steve Wunsch, Amazon Kindle, 2010, Kindle location 6280. This process and these terms, which were not invented by me, were described and lamented by many SEC critics from both the NYSE and Nasdaq during the 1980s and 1990s. In a sign of how thoroughly the SEC's takeover of market structure has extinguished the independence and creative autonomy of the private markets, both the episode and the terms are now largely forgotten, and never come up in today's market structure discussions. The only questions now revolve around things like how to manage the data demands and debacles of the clone-based market, e.g., how to avoid flash crashing and Knightmares. Forgotten, too, is that such things never used to happen when markets were distinct.

xl *Law, Legislation and Liberty, Vol. 2, The Mirage of Social Justice*, Friedrich A. Hayek, University of Chicago Press, 1976, pp. 108-109. "The market order serves no such single order of ends [as what is normally called an "economy" does]. What is commonly called a social or national economy is in this sense not a single economy but a network of many interlaced economies . . . [for which] we can form an English term *catallaxy* which we shall use to describe the order brought about by the mutual adjustment of many individual economies in a market. A catallaxy is thus the special kind of spontaneous order produced by the market through people acting within the rules of the law of property, tort and contract."

xli *Capitalism, Socialism and Democracy*, Joseph A. Schumpeter, 1943, Kindle version Mobipocket.com 2002/2003, Kindle location 1939. "The opening up of new markets, foreign or domestic, and the organizational development from the craft shop and factory to such concerns as U.S. Steel illustrate the same process of industrial mutation – if I may use that biological term – that incessantly revolutionizes the structure from within, incessantly destroying the old one, incessantly creating a new one. This process of Creative Destruction is the essential fact about capitalism. It is what capitalism consists in and what every capitalist concern has to live in."

xlii The *Kevin Bacon game* was popular in the early six-degrees-fascination phase, when it was found that a few super-connectors like Kevin Bacon, who played in many films, were responsible for a surprisingly small world among actors. The idea of the game was to connect a given actor to Kevin Bacon in the minimum number of steps by identifying a chain of casts that connected them. If Movie #1 had actors A and B in their casts, and Movie #2 had actors B and C, and Move #3 had Actor C and

Kevin Bacon, then there were three degrees of separation between Actor A and Kevin Bacon.

xliii *National Commission on Terrorist Attacks Upon the United States,* Thomas H. Kean, Lee H. Hamilton, August 21, 2004. "Much of the public commentary about the 9/11 attacks has dealt with "lost opportunities" . . . These are often characterized as problems of "watchlisting," of "information sharing," or of "connecting the dots." . . . These labels are too narrow. They describe the symptoms, not the disease."

xliv *The History of Rockland County,* p. 3; Frank Bertangue Green, M.D., Library of Congress, 1886.

xlv Wikipedia.

xlvi Origin: mid 16th cent.: via Latin from Greek monopolion, from monos 'single' + polein 'sell.' Apple dictionary. When the king granted you a monopoly, or sole seller privilege, that meant that it was illegal for anyone else to compete with you.

xlvii This was my impression of how things changed on the business process and electronic trading system front in the years from around 2004 to 2008, which, as a patent holder for the ISE's midpoint match stock exchange (US 20070055607), I had occasion to observe.

xlviii *In Silicon Valley, Patents Go on Trial: Tech Giants Near a Landmark Jury Trial over iPhone and Android: Is it Innovation or Litigation?* Ashby Jones, Jessica E. Vascellaro, Wall Street Journal, July 25, 2012.

xlix Having been involved in designing and launching trading systems businesses and stock exchanges for two decades, I had occasion to observe the value of intellectual property to such businesses, both for those I was involved in and for dozens of other businesses of friends, colleagues and competitors. Although I witnessed a few legal spats over IP, never did I see cases where the IP was determinative or even meaningful in terms of business success. While it was nice to brag about when raising money, it really didn't help shore up the business position or bring in that critical mass of customers. I witnessed no instance in which the primary or even secondary or tertiary motivation to invent came from the lure of IP protection of any kind, although I saw many examples in which lawyers advised spending maximum amounts on IP, just in case.

l *Samsung wins patent battle over Apple in Seoul,* Edmonton Journal, Reuters, August 24, 2012.

li *Tokyo Court Hands Win to Samsung Over Apple,* Hiroko Tabuchi, Nick Winfield, New York Times, September 1, 2012.

lii In an interview within days of the verdict (August 28, 2012) with Bloomberg West reporter Emily Chang, jury foreman Vel Hogan said his 9-member panel started out leaning one way, against Apple, and came out unanimous the other way, for Apple, largely, it appears, due to his personal ability to educate members in the intricacies of the law, which, being a patent holder himself, he was in a position to do. As to the rectangle with rounded corners question, he told Chang that it wasn't as simple as that, because there were many separate claims that all led when interpreted by designers to a full look and feel that just happened to come out as a rectangle with rounded corners. He did not explain how all those claims might have led to the same look and feel but with a different shape and, if they did not, how the situation he described was practically speaking any different from having a patent on a rectangle with rounded corners. He also did not address why such claims were upheld as an I-Phone patent, but rejected as an I-Pad patent.

liii *Justice Department Poised to Clear Google-Motorola Deal*, Thomas Catan, Ian Sherr, The Wall Street Journal, February 9, 2012.

liv *Tech Patents Soar in Value*, Shira Ovide, John Letzing, The Wall Street Journal, April 9, 2012.

lv The two ways they do this are, first, by alleging that monopolization does not really happen much anyway, because natural competition takes care of it (the "deregulation" argument), implying that their client wouldn't have bothered to try to monopolize, particularly not in such a competitive industry; or, second, by claiming that, while modern judges are misinterpreting original congressional intent, there is a correct interpretation that would usefully and constitutionally constrain monopolies (as Bork argues). Both of these arguments presume that, at least in some cases (not theirs, of course), antitrust is a correct and valid law. For a further discussion of the denial defense, see *Countdown*, Kindle location 1070 – 1105.

lvi *Strauss-Kahn Says Sex Parties Went Too Far, but Lust Is No Crime,* Doreen Carvajal, Maïa de la Baume, New York Times, October 14, 2012. "The exclusive orgies called "parties fines" – lavish Champagne affairs costing around $13,000 each – were organized as a roving international circuit from Paris to Washington by businessmen seeking to ingratiate themselves with Mr. Strauss-Kahn. Some of that money, according to a lawyer for the main host, ultimately paid for prostitutes because of a shortage of women at the mixed soirees orchestrated largely for the benefit of Mr. Strauss-Kahn, who sometimes sought sex with three or four women."

lvii *The Master Switch: The Rise and Fall of Information Empires,* Tim Wu, Knopf eBook, New York, 2010, Amazon Kindle, Kindle location 5720-5738. Wu, the originator of the net neutrality concept, argues for a Separations Principle, something more constitutional than regulatory, that would remove the FCC's traditional discretion to relax or not apply antitrust strictures.

lviii *Torturer's Apprentice*, Cullen Murphy, The Atlantic, January 2012.

lix *Cows, Pigs, Wars & Witches: The Riddles of Culture*, Marvin Harris, copyright 1974, Vintage Books, 1989, Amazon Kindle, Kindle location 2580.

lx "The term "witch-hunt" since the 1930s has also been in use as a metaphor to refer to moral panics in general (frantic persecution of perceived enemies)." Wikipedia.

lxi *Morgan: American Financier*, Jean Strouse, Random House, 1999, pp 674-680.

lxii *Titan: The Life of John D. Rockefeller, Sr.*, Ron Chernow, Random House, 1998. Chernow, who bought into the vilification narrative, nonetheless could not find, after much searching, evidence of any moral lapses. Further, since Rockefeller insisted that every one of his business methods was proper and ethical, Chernow could not pin the charge on him that his critics always had, namely that the great monopolist knew he was guilty of great sins and thus had been insincere in his protestations of innocence over the years. Instead, as Chernow said in his Foreword, "Rockefeller's life was of a piece . . . the pious, Bible-thumping Rockefeller wasn't simply a cunning façade for the corporate pirate. The religious and acquisitive sides of his nature were intimately related."

lxiii *Outliers: The Story of Success,* Malcolm Gladwell, Little, Brown and Company, 2008, Amazon Kindle, Kindle location 787-807. Note particularly the asterisked reference to sociologist C. Wright Mills (Kindle location 807) who says, "The best time during the history of the United States for the poor boy ambitions for high business success to have been born was around 1835." See also *War on Wealth: The SEC, the National Market System and the Flash Crash,* Steve Wunsch, Amazon Kindle, 2011, Kindle location 532-552. I take issue with Gladwell's assertion that the success of these richest people of all time was due to being born at a fortunate time. I argue that they largely created the "luck" they happened upon by creating new industries or extending old ones through monopolization. Their good fortune was being able to do so before the Sherman Act made such success illegal.

lxiv Wikipedia on "socialism"

lxv *The Age of Austerity: How Scarcity Will Remake American Politics*, Thomas Byrne Edsall, Doubleday, 2012, Amazon Kindle. Kindle location 266.

lxvi *The Social Atom: Why the Rich Get Richer, Cheaters Get Caught, and Your Neighbor Usually Looks Like You*, Mark Buchanan, Bloomsbury USA, 2007, Amazon Kindle. Kindle location 2194.

lxvii *World On Fire: How Exporting Free Market Democracy Breeds Ethnic Hatred and Global Instability*, Amy Chua, Doubleday, 2003, Amazon Kindle, Kindle location 145.

lxviii *Bird Flu Studies To Be Published Despite Concern*, Denise Grady, The New York Times, February 18, 2012.

lxix *Terror Fears Fail to Halt Study,* Christopher Weaver, Wall Street Journal, May 2, 2012.

lxx *Toward A New World Order*, President George H. W. Bush, speech to a joint session of Congress, September 11, 1990.

lxxi *Address to a joint session of Congress and the American People*, President George W. Bush, September 20, 2001.

lxxii *Hunting in the Shadows: The Pursuit of al Qa'ida Since 9/11,* Seth G. Jones, W. W. Norton, 2012, Amazon Kindle, Kindle location 7886.

lxxiii *Unwed Mothers Now A Majority Before Age of 30*, Jason Deparle, Sabrina Tavernise, The New York Times, February 18, 2012.

lxxiv The Syrian conflict where Secretary Clinton is evoking U.S. and "world" authority to oust the Assad regime, threatens to drag in neighbor Turkey, where similar ethnic and religious divisions exist, but so far with different balances and outcomes. Even if pluralism and democracy were solutions in the long run, our persistent preaching of them today is leading to conflict and dangers. *Turkey's Shiites Fear Contagion – As Hostilities Worsen between Ankara and Damascus, Minority Sects Worry the Tensions Next Door Will Spread*, Ayla Albaylak, Joe Parkinson, The Wall Street Journal, April 9, 2012.

lxxv *Polling the Occupy Wall Street Crowd*, Douglas Schoen, The Wall Street Journal, October 18, 2011.

lxxvi Wikipedia, "1883: The Death of Karl Marx," Marxists.org, retrieved 21 December, 2009.

lxxvii *Mutual Aid: A Factor of Evolution,* Pyotr Alexeyevich Kropotkin, 1902, Amazon Kindle, Kindle location 4160—4174.

lxxviii *Cows, Pigs, Wars and Witches: The Riddles of Culture*, Marvin Harris, Vintage Books, a division of Random House, 1974, Amazon Kindle, "Messiahs" and "The Secret of the Prince of Peace," Kindle locations 1777 and 2050, respectively.

lxxix The Air for tenor in Scene One of Handel's *Messiah* sings the words of the eighth century BC prophet Isaiah.

lxxx *Cows, Pigs, Wars and Witches: The Riddles of Culture,* Marvin Harris, Vintage Books, a division of Random House, 1974, Amazon Kindle, Kindle location 1545.

lxxxi *Cows, Pigs, Wars and Witches: The Riddles of Culture,* Marvin Harris, Vintage Books, a division of Random House, 1974, Amazon Kindle, Kindle location 2601.

lxxxii *Cows, Pigs, Wars and Witches: The Riddles of Culture,* Marvin Harris, Vintage Books, a division of Random House, 1974, Amazon Kindle, Kindle location 2620.

lxxxiii The salute was mandatory for civilians during Hitler's time, except for Jews, who were forbidden to use it. It is now forbidden for anyone to use it, except in satire.

lxxxiv *Seventeen Afghan partygoers beheaded by Taliban: Officials say 15 men and two women killed as punishment for attending a mixed-sex party with music and dancing,* Reuters, The Guardian, August 27, 2012.

lxxxv *Cows, Pigs, Wars and Witches: The Riddles of Culture,* Marvin Harris, Vintage Books, a division of Random House, 1974, Amazon Kindle, "Primitive War," "The Savage Male," Kindle locations 709 and 958, respectively. Harris describes how some primitive peoples that still exist and can be observed by scientists conduct war in very scripted ways, as if they were sports contests with deadly consequences and territorial gain or loss as a result. They included a short break upon the first injury and one or two days at the first death for potential reconciliation, as well as about twelve years of peace between wars.

lxxxvi *Cows, Pigs, Wars and Witches: The Riddles of Culture,* Marvin Harris, Vintage Books, a division of Random House, 1974, Amazon Kindle, "Primitive War," "The Savage Male," Kindle locations 709 and 958, respectively. Harris speculates that the evolutionary value of the wars was to avoid overpopulation that would grow a people beyond the ability of its forest environment to support them. Surprisingly, the primary way population is limited is not through the deaths of males in war, although there are many of those, but through infanticide of females, which severely retards the ability of the population to grow. Such infanticide, combined with the brutality of males toward females and other males, worked together to both win wars for individual tribes and to limit population for the overall society of all the tribes.

lxxxvii *Mutual Aid: A Factor of Evolution,* Pyotr Alexeyevich Kropotkin, 1902, Amazon Kindle, Kindle location 5: "Two aspects of animal life impressed me most during the journeys which I made in my youth in Eastern Siberia and Northern Manchuria. One of them was the extreme severity of the struggle for existence which most species of animals have to carry on against an inclement Nature; the enormous destruction of life which periodically results from natural agencies; and the consequent paucity of life over the vast territory which fell under my observation. And the other was, that even in those few spots where animal life teemed in abundance, I failed to find – although I was eagerly looking for it – that bitter struggle for the means of existence, among animals of the same species, which was considered by most Darwinists (though not always by Darwin himself) as the dominant characteristic of struggle for life, and the main factor of evolution." "On the other hand, wherever I saw animal life in abundance . . . I saw Mutual Aid and Mutual Support carried on to an extent which made me suspect in it a feature of the greatest importance for the maintenance of life, the preservation of each species, and its further evolution." [Kindle location 26–30]

lxxxviii *Mutual Aid: A Factor of Evolution*, Pyotr Alexeyevich Kropotkin, 1902, Amazon Kindle, Kindle location 1155: "Now, if we take into consideration that this complicated [clan] organization developed among men who stood at the lowest known degree of development, and that it maintained itself in societies knowing no kind of authority besides the authority of public opinion, we at once see how deeply inrooted social instincts must have been in human nature, even at its lowest stages. A savage who is capable of living under such an organization, and of freely submitting to rules which continually clash with his personal desires, certainly is not a beast devoid of ethical principles and knowing no rein to its passions."

lxxxix *The True Cost of the Iraq War: $3 Trillion and Beyond*, Joseph E. Stiglitz, Linda J. Bilmes, The Washington Post, September 5, 2010.

xc *Freedom and Restraint,* John Fabian Witt, The New York Times, September 22, 2012.

xci *Lincoln's Code: The Laws of War in American History*, John Fabian Witt, Free Press, Amazon Kindle, Kindle location 162.

xcii *Lincoln's Code: The Laws of War in American History*, John Fabian Witt, Free Press, Amazon Kindle, Kindle location 4565. "For months, Confederate authorities had been warning that Emancipation would mark the beginning of a Union effort to foment slave uprisings across the South. Now the white inhabitants of Jacksonville – "in mortal dread of the sable soldiers," as one correspondent reported – expected an indiscriminate massacre. Around the country, observers expected that raids such as the one led by the South Carolina Volunteers would be "like a great volcano . . . bursting" upon the South. Critics of the Lincoln administration in the North condemned the expedition (the "wretched business of negro soldiering") as war "against women and children on the plantations, and not against armed force in the field.""

xciii *Lincoln's Code: The Laws of War in American History*, John Fabian Witt, Free Press, Amazon Kindle, Kindle location 5103. ""The employment of a servile insurrection as an instrument of war," Secretary [of War James] Seddon argued, "is contrary to the usages of civilized nations." In "the better days of the Republic," he maintained, the Untied States "would have regarded an attempt of the kind as dishonoring to the State or people who might be guilty of adopting it. ""The South's counter-atrocities included summary executions of black soldiers and their commanding white officers and, in the case of the black soldiers, returning them to their former masters or selling them to new masters, a practice that resulted in selling into bondage some blacks who had been free before they became Union soldiers. The South refused to treat captured black soldiers as prisoners of war, whether they had been slaves or free before the war, a distinction that made them ineligible for prisoner exchanges. The dispute over what constituted civilized war led to a stalemate over prisoner exchanges that was said to have resulted in 100 unnecessary deaths a day among prisoners who could have been exchanged, but weren't [Kindle location 5411].

xciv *Freedom and Restraint,* John Fabian Witt, The New York Times, September 22, 2012.

xcv *Freedom and Restraint,* John Fabian Witt, The New York Times, September 22, 2012.

xcvi *Taliban Reiterate Vow to Kill Pakistani Girl,* Declan Walsh, New York Times, October 13, 2012. "The police said Friday that they had made several arrests in connection with the Taliban's shooting of Malala Yousafzai, a 14-year-old education activist who was critically injured, but militant commanders in northwestern Pakistan reiterated their intention to kill the schoolgirl or her father." The article was referenced in a caption at the bottom of a large front-page picture of children in white shirts and ties praying for the girl who was shot "for promoting education for girls."

xcvii *Afghan Army's High Turnover Clouds U.S. Exit Plan,* Rod Nordland, New York Times, October 15, 2012. "The Afghan deserters complain of corruption among their officers, poor food and equipment, indifferent medical care, Taliban intimidation of their families and, probably most troublingly, a lack of belief in the army's ability to fight the insurgents after the American military withdraws."

xcviii *Cows, Pigs, Wars and Witches: The Riddles of Culture,* Marvin Harris, Vintage Books, a division of Random House, 1974, Amazon Kindle, Kindle location 734.

xcix *The 5000 Year Leap: 28 Great Ideas That Changed the World,* W. Cleon Skousen, American Documents Publishing, 1981; *Ameritopia: the Unmaking of America,* Mark R. Levin, Threshold Editions, 2012.

c *Crisis and Leviathan: Critical Episodes in the Growth of American Government,* Robert Higgs, Oxford Press, 1987, p.60.

ci "One typical course of medical treatment began the morning of 13 July 1824. A French sergeant was stabbed through the chest while engaged in single combat; within minutes, he fainted from loss of blood. Arriving at the local hospital he was immediately bled twenty ounces (570 ml) "to prevent inflammation." During the night he was bled another 24 ounces (680 ml). Early the next morning, the chief surgeon bled the patient another 10 ounces (285 ml); during the next 14 hours he was bled five more times. Medical attendants thus intentionally removed more than half of the patient's normal blood supply – in addition to the initial blood loss which caused the sergeant to faint. Bleedings continued over the next several days. By 29 July, the wound had become inflamed. The physician applied 32 leeches to the most sensitive part of the wound. Over the next three days, there were more bleedings and a total of 40 more leeches. The sergeant recovered and was released on 3 October. His physician wrote that "by the large quantity of blood lost, amounting to 170 ounces [nearly eleven pints] (4.8 liters), besides that drawn by the application of leeches [perhaps another two pints] (1.1 liters), the life of the patient was preserved." By nineteenth-century standards, thirteen pints of blood taken over the space of a month was a large but not exceptional quantity. The medical literature of the period contains many similar accounts – some successful, some not." Wikipedia.

[cii] *More Americans Live in Economically Segregated Neighborhoods than 30 Years Ago,* PBS Newshour interview by Gwen Ifill of Paul Taylor of the Pew Research Center, August 1, 2012.

[ciii] The Constitution was adopted on September 17, 1787, ratified on June 21, 1788 and went into effect on March 4, 1789. Wikipedia.

[civ] Contained in the First Amendment of our Bill of Rights, which are the first ten amendments to our Constitution.

[cv] Wikipedia.

[cvi] Chomsky's claim of an innate universal grammar (UG) is, according to critics, an English-centric conclusion that is not supported if many languages' learning processes are looked at. Wikipedia.

[cvii] Schopenhauer, *Parerga and Paralipomena*, Vol. 1, Section 13. Wikipedia: Fichte.

[cviii] Wikipedia.

[cix] *History of the Philosophy of Mind*, Vol. 4, p. 114, Robert Blakely, Longmans: London, 1850. Wikipedia.

[cx] Wikipedia: Fichte.

[cxi] Wikipedia: Fichte.

[cxii] *Letter to Edward Carrington*, Thomas Jefferson, Paris, May 27, 1788.

[cxiii] *The Antitrust Paradox: A Policy at War with Itself.* Robert H. Bork, Basic Books, Inc., 1978, p. 26.

[cxiv] *SEC's Schapiro: Circuit Breakers Contained Knight Capital Damage,* Justin Grant, Advanced Trading Magazine, August 3, 2012. "'Existing rules make it clear that when broker-dealers with access to our markets use computers to trade, to trade fast, or to trade frequently, they must check those systems to ensure they're operating properly,' she [SEC Chairman Mary Schapiro] said. 'Naturally, we will consider whether such compliance measures were followed in this case.'"

[cxv] In Hitler's Germany, the *Endlösung,* or "final solution to the Jewish question" was the secret plan to exterminate Jews in death camps.

[cxvi] Wikipedia. Adolf Hitler addressing the German Reichstag, January 30, 1939.

[cxvii] Wikipedia. *Gesamtausgabe*, Vol. I/1, pp. 292-293.

[cxviii] Stab-in-the-back myth (*Dolchstosslegende).* Wikipedia.

[cxix] *Into the Cannibal's Pot: Lessons for America from Post-Apartheid South Africa,* Ilana Mercer, Stairway Press, Seattle, 2011, Amazon Kindle, Kindle location 1238.

[cxx] "Many diplomats, like the United States' then-secretary of state Warren Christopher, refused to call the actions "genocide" for fear the United Nations Genocide Convention would require greater action. These actions, and the silence of the world despite many news reports of the killings, led the extremist Hutus to act with a feeling of impunity." Holocaust Museum Houston.

[cxxi] In German, *Deutsche Arbeiterpartei.*

[cxxii] In German, *Nationalsozialistische Deutsche Arbeiterpartei, NSDAP* (National Socialist German Workers Party, NSGWP).

cxxiii *The Age of Austerity: How Scarcity will Remake American Politics*, Thomas Byrne Edsall, Doubleday, a division of Random House, 2012, Amazon Kindle, Kindle location 1918. Edsall provides numerous examples of how better economic environments create more tolerant attitudes toward minorities and immigrants and, conversely, how recessions cause intolerance to re-emerge, such as in Arizona most recently.

cxxiv *The Real Lincoln: A New Look at Abraham Lincoln, His Agenda and an Unnecessary War*, Thomas DiLorenzo, Three Rivers Press, New York, 2002. Amazon Kindle, 2009, Kindle location 165.

cxxv Apple dictionary. Chivalry: "the combination of qualities expected of an ideal knight, esp. courage, honor, courtesy, justice, and a readiness to help the weak."

cxxvi CNBC, October 16, 2012.

cxxvii On NBC's Meet the Press, May 15, 2011, Gingrich told David Gregory: "I don't think right wing social engineering is any more desirable than left wing social engineering. I don't think imposing radical change from the right or the left is a very good way for a free society to operate. I think we need a national conversation to get to a better Medicare system with more choices for seniors." Gingrich's critique of the Ryan plan was on point, as this favorable review of the Ryan plan in the Wall Street Journal accidentally proves: *The Forgotten History of Ryan's Medicare Reform,* Joseph Rago, the Wall Street Journal, August 13, 2012. But there is no reason to think his "national conversation" will lead to anything less socialist than the Ryan plan or Obamacare. They all amount to social engineering, or what I call economic eugenics.

cxxviii *Investor Interests as the Common Interest: The SEC Campaign for Fair Trading Practices,* SEC Chairman Arthur Levitt speech to the Economic Club of Chicago, April 24 1996. I noted and further discussed this comment in *War on Wealth*, Kindle Location 625.

cxxix *The trouble with small tick sizes*, David Weild, Edward Kim, Lisa Newport, Grant Thornton Capital Markets Series paper. "In today's stock market structure, most small companies' exit strategies no longer include a public listing, but rather a merger or acquisition. When these companies cannot raise capital effectively through the IPO market, they must look to a merger or acquisition, and jobs are lost, not gained. This represents an opportunity cost of millions of jobs and untapped economic growth. We estimate that this dearth of IPOs has cost the United States as many as 9.4 million additional jobs that might have been created after companies go public. If we add the private market effect (our best estimate of the multiplier effect in the private market when more companies go public), the number of additional jobs increases to 18.8 million."

cxxx *Dark Pool Comment Letter,* Steve Wunsch, Amazon Kindle, 2010, Kindle location 564. The letter is also available on the SEC's Website at http://www.sec.gov/comments/s7-27-09/s72709-32.pdf

cxxxi *War on Wealth,* Steve Wunsch, Amazon Kindle, 2011, Kindle location 642.

cxxxii *Dark Pool Comment Letter,* Steve Wunsch, Amazon Kindle, 2010, Kindle location 172-213. The letter is also available on the SEC's Website at http://www.sec.gov/comments/s7-27-09/s72709-32.pdf

cxxxiii *Countdown,* Steve Wunsch, 2001, Amazon Kindle, 2010, Kindle location 641-649.

cxxxiv *Publishers' Favorite President: Four Score and 16,000 Books,* Stefanie Cohen, The Wall Street Journal, October 12, 2012. ""He saved the American dream, and he lived the American dream," says Harold Holzer, a Lincoln historian who has written and edited 42 books about the man."

cxxxv *Lincoln Unmasked: What You're Not Supposed to know about Dishonest Abe,* Thomas DiLorenzo, Three Rivers Press, 2007. Kindle edition, 2009, Kindle location 453-495.

cxxxvi *Lincoln Unmasked: What You're Not Supposed to Know About Dishonest Abe,* Thomas DiLorenzo, Three Rivers Press, 2007. Amazon Kindle, 2009, Kindle location 1643. Lincoln was catapulted to the presidency for his constant support of high tariffs, which he promised to and did increase further during his administration. This hurt agricultural exporters in the South. The combination of the Lincoln-supported Morrill Tariff, which increased rates by about 70% and went into effect two days before Lincoln took office, his promises to increase tariffs further, and his promise in his first inaugural address to force collection of the tariffs with military action [Kindle location 1691], set off the secession of southern states. "When protectionist tariffs cause a reduction in imports (which is their sole purpose), our foreign trading partners will then have fewer dollars with which to buy our exported goods to their countries—especially agricultural products. Restricting imports today will invariably cause a reduction of our own exports tomorrow. And remember, the mid-nineteenth-century South had an overwhelmingly export-oriented economy. The South exported as much as three-fourths of what it produced and was economically devastated by high protectionist tariffs" [Kindle location 1618].

cxxxvii *Lincoln Unmasked: What You're Not Supposed to know about Dishonest Abe,* Thomas DiLorenzo, Three Rivers Press, 2007. Amazon Kindle edition 2009, Kindle location 390 ff: *The Myth of the Morally Superior "Yankee."*

cxxxviii *Second Inaugural Address,* President Abraham Lincoln, March 4, 1865.

cxxxix *Lincolnian Totalitarians,* Thomas DiLorenzo, copyright LewRockwell.com, 2004. "This of course is why totalitarians of all stripes have always lionized Lincoln. In *Mein Kampf* (1996 Houghton-Mifflin edition, p. 566), Adolf Hitler paraphrased the (false) theory that Lincoln introduced in his first inaugural address that no such thing as states' rights ever existed in America to make *his* case for the abolition of states' rights in Germany."

cxl Abraham Lincoln's Letter to Horace Greeley, August 22, 1862.

cxli These calls were first forced on Archipelago as a quid pro quo that allowed it to become an exchange by merging with the Pacific Stock Exchange. The NYSE later bought Archipelago as part of the Big Board's plan to become a public company, and gradually replaced its manual specialist auction with Archipelago's electronic model at the SEC's urging. Nasdaq was forced to adopt the SEC's model, too, also as a quid pro quo when it needed Commission acquiescence to several key related plans, such as to operate a new electronic platform, to convert from a mutual dealer association to a demutualized exchange, and to go public. Prior to this, Nasdaq did not have an electronic open or close at all, much less a single price call auction, but merely started or stopped quoting by its dealers at opening or closing times. None of these markets wanted to adopt the SEC's model, or considered it superior to what they already had or could design and build themselves. In fact, all of them had at various times strongly resisted electronic calls. But all of them bowed to the SEC's wishes in order to obtain approval for things like exchange licenses, mergers, demutualizing or going public. NMS created desperate needs for all markets to quickly gain such critical path permissions simply in order to survive, and thus created powerful leverage for the SEC's quid pro quos. However strange or counterproductive the Commission's call market rules seemed, acquiescing to them without debate was a small price to pay for these permissions.

cxlii "Nasdaq officials said Sunday that they confronted a problem they hadn't anticipated in test runs. They said trading volume in Facebook wasn't more than anticipated. But because of the size of the Facebook IPO and the level of investor interest, the process of matching up buy and sell orders to pinpoint the price of the first trade took slightly longer than normal—five milliseconds instead of three, according to Mr. Greifeld." *Nasdaq's Facebook Problem,* Jenny Strasburg, Jason Bunge, Gina Chon, Wall Steet Journal, May 21, 2012.

cxliii *Facebook: The Strangest IPO of All Time?* Ivy Schmerken, Wall Street and Technology Magazine, May 24, 2012. "The botched [Facebook] IPO at Nasdaq comes on the heels of electronic stock exchange operator BATS Global Markets having to withdraw its own IPO after a software glitch surfaced in March. In BATS's case the company successfully completed the auction but had trouble transitioning to continuous trading when the technology bug surfaced. According to Nasdaq's own post-mortem on what happened with the Facebook electronic IPO, it ran into problems when it was attempting to end the quoting period and execute the IPO cross, matching buyers and sellers, and print the opening trade. As the software was recalculating the opening price, additional order modifications were received by the system. The problems took place within a 5 millisecond window, according to a story in Monday's Financial Times. "Because of a decision before to allow continuous order placement during IPOs, cancellations kept 'fitting in between the raindrops,'" during the 5 milliseconds it was taking to determine a price, in the words of [Nasdaq CEO Bob] Greifeld. The fact that Nasdaq talked about a 5 millisecond window is not surprising in the world of trading today. "Those are the time windows that decisions are made in, [and] quite frankly [could be] much faster than that," says Azul System's [CEO Scott] Sellers. For computers and programs that trade, 5 milliseconds is a long time, he says. "You have to realize that an Intel microprocessor calculates 2.5 billion operations per second, so within 5 milliseconds you can still have 10 million calculations," he estimates. "You can imagine how many trades were going on in that time frame.""

cxliv *Are Dads the New Mom's?* Susan Gregory Thomas, Wall Street Journal, May 11, 2012.

cxlv *U.S. May Scrap Costly Effort to Train Iraqi Police,* Tim Arango, New York Times, May 13, 2012.

cxlvi *U.S. Relaxes Drone Rules,* Adam Entous, Siobhan Gorman, Julian E. Barnes, The Wall Street Journal, April 26, 2012.

cxlvii Even the Civil War's 620,000 deaths, if adjusted for population changes since then, would have produced 5 million deaths, according to DiLorenzo in *The Real Lincoln*, Kindle location 168.

cxlviii *HFT and the Hidden Cost of Deep Liquidity,* Pragma Securities, Tabbforum.com, July 30, 2012.

cxlix *SEC's Schapiro: Circuit Breakers Contained Knight Capital Damage,* Justin Grant, Advanced Trading Magazine, August 3, 2012. "'Recently-adopted circuit breakers halted trading on individual stocks that experienced significant price fluctuations, and clearly defined rules guided the exchanges in determining which trades could be broken, giving the marketplace certainty,' Schapiro said in a statement. She added that the SEC is reviewing the incident and is looking into whether or not additional regulatory steps should be taken to shore up the market."

cl *Lawmakers Push for Overhaul of IPO Process,* Jean Eaglesham, Telis Demos, Wall Street Journal, June 21, 2012. The article highlights a letter from Congressman Darrell Issa to SEC Chairman Mary Schapiro pointedly asking (in question 31) why the Commission would not require Dutch auctions (a form of call auction used in the Google IPO) instead of underwriter-set prices for IPOs.

cli *Lincoln Unmasked: What You're Not Supposed to Know About Dishonest Abe*, Thomas DiLorenzo, Three Rivers Press, 2007. Amazon Kindle, 2009, Kindle location 1643. Lincoln was catapulted to the presidency for his constant support of high tariffs, which he promised to and did increase further during his administration. This hurt agricultural exporters in the South. The combination of the Lincoln-supported Morrill Tariff, which increased rates by about 70% and went into effect two days before Lincoln took office, his promises to increase tariffs further, and his promise in his first inaugural address to force collection of the tariffs with military action [Kindle location 1691], set off the secession of southern states. "When protectionist tariffs cause a reduction in imports (which is their sole purpose), our foreign trading partners will then have fewer dollars with which to buy our exported goods to their countries—especially agricultural products. Restricting imports today will invariably cause a reduction of our own exports tomorrow. And remember, the mid-nineteenth-century South had an overwhelmingly export-oriented economy. The South exported as much as three-fourths of what it produced and was economically devastated by high protectionist tariffs" [Kindle location 1618].

clii As Thomas Jefferson warned in his 1801 inaugural address, in which he recommended "peace, commerce and honest friendship with all nations, entangling alliances with none."

cliii Charles-Louis de Secondat, baron de Brède et La Montesquieu, 1689-1755.

cliv *The Real Lincoln: A New Look at Abraham Lincoln, His Agenda and an Unnecessary War,* Thomas DiLorenzo, Three River Press, New York, 2002. Kindle edition, 2009, Kindle location 168. *Lincoln Unmasked: What You're Not Supposed to Know About Dishonest Abe,* Thomas DiLorenzo, Three Rivers Press, 2006. Kindle edition, 2009, Kindle locations 279 and 729.

clv The Espionage Act of 1917, as amended by the Sedition Act of 1918. Wikipedia.

clvi *SEC Looks to Tighten Trading Controls,* Andrew Ackerman, Scott Patterson, the Wall Street Journal, August 7, 2012. "Now regulators want to fix a crucial shortcoming: the [ARP] policies aren't currently enforceable. SEC officials are considering naming the new rule SCI, for "systems compliance and integrity," according to people familiar with the matter. Ms. Schapiro first called for the guidance to become mandatory in a March 2011 speech, saying newer technology should lead to stronger rules."

clvii My analysis was laid out in eight articles I wrote in the months after the Flash Crash. The articles are in Appendix I of *War on Wealth*, Kindle location 869. *Straitjacket*, the last and most detailed of them, starts at Kindle location 1350.

clviii As one of those involved in the Reg. NMS rollout, I too could have asked about stub quotes and stop orders. But it didn't occur to me then, although I was familiar with each of them as well as Reg. NMS and could have easily imagined their toxic interaction if I had but thought of it. That is why from late afternoon on the day of the Flash Crash I was pretty sure how it happened, and, since I knew that many others had at least the same experience and knowledge base I had, I thought many others understood the problem, too, and would soon be saying so. That none of them did became part of the narrative I chronicled in my articles referenced in the previous footnote. To this day, although many have told me privately I had it right from the beginning, none has spoken up publicly or challenged the SEC's self-defensive interpretation of events.

clix Comment made by Commissioner Daniel M. Gallagher when questioning industry experts addressing ARP at the SEC's Technology and Trading Roundtable: *Promoting Stability in Today's Market*, on October 2, 2012.

clx *Despite Gains, Many Flee Stock Market*, E. S. Browning, The Wall Street Journal, October 5, 2012. "Some clients say they no longer trust Wall Street. ""I [a broker] get the reaction, they are all a bunch of thieves and liars and you can't trust them," he said. "The news flow continues to reinforce it."" "A pullback from stocks leaves trading increasingly in the hands of professionals—hedge funds and high-frequency traders that use hard-to-regulate computerized methods. That makes the market more volatile, helping fuel events such as the "flash crash" on May 6, 2010, when the Dow Jones Industrial Average fell 700 points in eight minutes. A decade ago, high-speed trading made up a small share of stock trading. Today, many large companies do little else, holding shares for as little as a second. They now represent more than half of all stock trades, according to Tabb Group, which tracks such transactions."

clxi *How Capitalism Saved America, Chapter 7, The Truth About the "Robber Barons,"* Thomas DiLorenzo, Ludwig von Mises Institute, Alfred A. Knopf, 2004.

clxii *Law, Legislation and Liberty, Vol. 3, The Political Order of a Free People*, Friedrich A. Hayek, 1979, p. 85. "Though it would not be desirable to make all discrimination illegal, aimed discrimination intended to enforce a certain market conduct should clearly be prohibited." I discuss this further in *Countdown,* Kindle location 288.

clxiii *World On Fire: How Exporting Free Market Democracy Breeds Ethnic Hatred and Global Instability,* Amy Chua, Doubleday, 2003, Amazon Kindle, Anchor Books, Random House Digital, Inc., January 6, 2004, Kindle location 3293.

clxiv *World On Fire,* Amy Chua, Kindle location 4900 ff. Chua prefaces her list of the mostly voluntary redistribution ideas she thinks could work or have worked, with the suggestions of Pulitzer Prize-winning author Jared Diamond, who "urges Americans to combat the forces of poverty and hopelessness on which international terrorism feeds through three basic strategies: providing health care, supporting family planning, and addressing chronic environmental problems such as deforestation that infuriate local populations." She also lauds former U.S. Treasury Secretary Robert Rubin, who "has called for an international campaign to raise public support for increased aid budgets, particularly in the United States," and former World Bank President James Wolfensohn, former UN Secretary General Kofi Annan and former British Chancellor of the Exchequer (and later Prime Minister) Gordon Brown for their proposal "calling for a $50 billion increase in foreign aid to poor countries, calling it "an insurance policy against future terrorism.""

clxv *Nantucket and Whaling,* PBS – The Voyage of the Odyssey – Class from the Sea – Ocean History.

clxvi *History of the American Whale Fishery,* Alexander Starbuck, Castle Books, 1989, pp. 95-96. "Nantucket, which during the War of 1812 had had its fleet of whale-ships reduced from forty-six to twenty-three, by the last of December, 1820, possessed seventy-five whale-ships, (with an aggregate of 20,449 tons,) besides several brigs, schooners and sloops. The same success which had advanced Nantucket so rapidly served to stimulate other ports, and New York, Long Island, New London, Cape Cod, Boston, and more particularly New Bedford, entered more vigorously into competition, and but a few years elapsed before the latter port, which was an offshoot, a child as it were of Nantucket, had far outstripped the extremest growth of the parent."

clxvii "Some researchers believe that by the 1860s whalemen may have reduced the world's sperm-whale population by as much as 75%; others claim that it was diminished by only 8 to 18 percent." *In the Heart of the Sea: The Tragedy of the Whaleship* Essex, Nathaniel Philbrick, Penguin Books, 2000, Amazon Kindle, Kindle Location 3633.

clxviii *History of the American Whale Fishery,* Alexander Starbuck, Castle Books, 1989, p. 110. "The expense of procuring oil was yearly increasing when the oil-wells of Pennsylvania were opened, and a source of illumination opened at once plentiful, cheap and good. Its dangerous qualities at first greatly checked its general use, but, these removed, it entered into active relentless competition with whale-oil, and it proved the more powerful of the antagonistic forces. The length of voyages increased from two years for a cargo of sperm and from nine to fifteen months for a cargo of whale-oil to four years to fill the latter, while the former was practically abandoned as a separate business after it became necessary to make voyages of four, five, and even six years, and then seldom return with a full cargo."

clxix *How Capitalism Saved America, Chapter 7, The Truth About the "Robber Barons",* Thomas DiLorenzo, Ludwig von Mises Institute, Alfred A. Knopf, 2004. "Once the refinery is built, the costs of maintaining the refinery are more or less fixed, so as more and more customers are added, the cost per customer declines. As a result, the company cut its cost of refining a gallon of oil from 3 cents in 1869 to less than half a cent by 1885. Significantly, Rockefeller passed these savings along to the consumer, as the price of refined oil plummeted from more than 30 cents per gallon in 1869 to 10 cents in 1874 and 8 cents in 1885."

clxx This was an "outlier" result that was also noted by Malcolm Gladwell in a best-selling book (*Outliers*, Malcolm Gladwell, Little Brown and Company, Hachette Book Group, 2008, Amazon Kindle, Kindle location 787). I have also mentioned, as did Gladwell, how their feat was not matched by anyone before or since, and how they often came from modest beginnings or poverty. Gladwell did not highlight the Robber Baron connection, but noted that the list of the wealthiest people in world history began at the top with an extraordinarily large number of Americans born between 1831 and 1840, a result that was extremely unlikely to have been caused by chance. That cohort happens to coincide with the Robber Baron cohort, such as Rockefeller (1839), Carnegie (1835) and Morgan (1837), the number 1, number 2 and number 57 wealthiest people of all time, respectively. I attribute their success not to the luck of their time of birth, but to their freedom to work hard at developing monopolies in the age before the Sherman Antitrust Act put a stop to such activities. While their successes no doubt reverberated off each other, and created opportunities for others who lived in their era, the greatest fortunes – e.g., Rockefeller's and Carnegie's – were created virtually single handedly by men who were born poor.

clxxi *Industry Comes of Age: Business, Labor and Public Policy, 1860 – 1897,* Edward C. Kirkland, 1961, pp 400 – 405. Wikipedia: the Gilded Age.

clxxii The Rise and Fall of the Great Powers, Paul Kennedy, 1987, p. 242. Wikipedia: The Gilded Age.

clxxiii Wikipedia: The Gilded Age.

clxxiv *The Rise and Fall of the Great Powers,* Paul Kennedy, 1987, p. 243. Wikipedia: The Gilded Age.

clxxv They believe that monopolies fail to maximize "consumer surplus" by maximizing production, and are therefore inefficient compared to their ideal of an economy that is running full tilt on all fronts all the time. I address the flaws in this traditional antitrust theory in various places in my writing, such as in *Mayday, Mayday, Countdown* and *War on Wealth*. For our purposes at this point in this work, the takeaway is that restraining monopolists produces far greater gaps in economic performance than the alleged gaps that their "restraints of trade" can possibly produce. If antitrust had always been successful at eliminating monopolies, it would have eliminated everything that has made America great economically. Fortunately, antitrust didn't exist before 1890, and has not been able to eliminate all monopolization since then, either. So the sun has shone through the antitrust clouds sufficiently to demonstrate the benefits that its elimination might produce.

clxxvi Like Herfindahl indexes, an antitrust regulation tool that measures the "contestability" of markets based on the number of competitors in them and their market shares, thereby supposedly telling regulators when to add more competition because a monopoly condition may exist.

clxxvii *NYSE to Pay $5 million Penalty to SEC,* Jenny Strasburg, Scott Patterson, Wall Street Journal, September 14, 2012. While the article mentions the NYSE's failure to include regulatory personnel in technology meetings that focused on delivery of data to customers, it did not get into the details. For example, it did not mention that, no matter what the exchange does, it is impossible to make the consolidated data delivered on the SEC's mandated "tape" arrive at the same time as the data distributed on private feeds, if for no other reason than that the tape must process and consolidate all the data from the exchanges before sending it out. Furthermore, no data tape, public or private, can possibly match the timely information high frequency traders get from markets' reactions to their own quotes and orders. So, no matter what the markets and the SEC do, the high frequency environment will always have some people with information advantages that others don't have. That was true of manual block trading, too. But then it was more obvious that merely mandating the elimination of the discrepancy by, for example, requiring an electronic level playing field, will never work. The impossibility of what the Commission is seeking this time, however, will not keep the Commission from milking the fines and fees it can assess as regulated entities inevitably fall into its traps.

[clxxviii] *NYSE Executive Urges Assessment of 2007 Stock Trading Overhaul,* Nina Mehta, Bloomberg News, September 20, 2012. "U.S. regulators and securities professionals should re-examine rules implemented in 2007 that transformed stock trading in the U.S., according to a NYSE Euronext executive. The proliferation of venues where investors can buy and sell shares, advances in trading speed spurred by computers, and the use of increasingly complex orders by high-frequency firms warrant a coordinated assessment, Joseph Mecane, head of U.S. Equities at NYSE Euronext, said at a conference yesterday. The analysis should focus on Regulation NMS, the set of rules meant to foster competition and speed trading in shares listed on the New York Stock Exchange, he said . . . The SEC should arrange a "series of market structure roundtables to discuss a lot of these items as an industry and to have a holistic recommendation or series of legislative changes coming out of these issues," Mecane said. "Each of these items is interrelated. I don't think they get addressed, largely because you can't address them in isolation.""

[clxxix] I discussed in particular the futility of market maker obligations in the new electronic environment in an article on October 19, 2010 in Advanced Trading Magazine, called *Market Maker Obligations for High-Frequency Traders are Not the Answer.* The article is also included in Appendix I of my book *War on Wealth* under the title, *Humpty Dumpty*, Amazon Kindle Location 1276.

[clxxx] *For Superfast Traders, A Way to Jump Ahead in Line,* Scott Patterson, Jenny Strasburg, Wall Street Journal, September 19, 2012.

[clxxxi] Only the best or top-of-book orders at each exchange are required to be "protected," i.e., not traded through, and are routed to as Intermarket Sweep Orders (ISOs) to satisfy Reg. NMS. Non-top-of-book orders at an exchange are not protected, even though they may be better priced than orders on other exchanges that do trade. This can lead to situations where better-priced but not protected orders on market A are quickly traded through on market B, but then cause volatility as they come into play immediately after that worse price trade on market B.

clxxxii *Industry Officials Call for Talks Around Order Types*, Peter Chapman, Trader's Magazine, November 5, 2012.